# TABLE OF

STUDYING AND OBEYING GOD'S WORD ONE PASSAGE AT A TIME

# Study James:
# 9 Practical Lessons
# On Living Out
# Your Faith

## *Jason Dexter*
### Author and General Editor

Study James: 9 Practical Lessons On Living Out Your Faith
Copyright © 2023 by Jason Dexter
All rights reserved

**Study and Obey**

# James 1:1-11

## Outline

I. Greetings (1)
II. Persevere in trials (2-4)
III. Pray with faith (5-8)
IV. Be humble and content (9-11)

## Authorship

Only two real candidates have been proposed, James, the brother of John, and James, the oldest and half-brother of Jesus (Mark 6:3). James, the brother of John, was probably martyred too early to have written this book, leaving James, Jesus' half-brother, as the author. He originally rejected Jesus as the Messiah but evidently trusted in Him after seeing Jesus resurrected (1 Corinthians 15:7). James was an associate of the apostles and a key leader in the Jerusalem church (Acts 12:17, Galatians 2:12).

## Background

The book of James was primarily directed towards Jewish believers who had been scattered, perhaps because of persecution under Herod Agrippa. As such, it is very Jewish in nature and contains frequent references to the Old Testament.

## Content

This epistle mostly focuses on practical Christian living as opposed to theoretical knowledge or doctrines. It concentrates on day-to-day life, relationship, and applications in the world around us. Its first aim seems to be to encourage the believers to live godly lives.

# I. Greetings (1)

## Discussion Questions

- Who is the author? What do you know about him?
- What is his relationship to God?
- Who are the recipients?

## Cross-References

Mark 6:3 – Isn't this the carpenter? Isn't this Mary's son and the brother of James, Joseph, Judas and Simon? Aren't his sisters here with us?" And they took offense at him.

1 Corinthians 15:7 – Then he appeared to James, then to all the apostles.

Acts 12:17 - Peter motioned with his hand for them to be quiet and described how the Lord had brought him out of prison. "Tell James and the other brothers and sisters about this," he said, and then he left for another place.

Galatians 2:12 – For before certain men came from James, he used to eat with the Gentiles. But when they arrived, he began to draw back and separate himself from the Gentiles because he was afraid of those who belonged to the circumcision group.

## Teaching Points

1. Who is James? - James is the half-brother of Jesus. He was the leader of the early New Testament church in Jerusalem. Also, he was one of the key people who decided on how to solve the conflict between the Gentiles and the Jews at the Council of Jerusalem.

The book is written primarily to a Jewish audience; hence it says, "to the twelve tribes scattered among the nations."

4

# II. Persevere in trials (2-4)

## Discussion Questions

- How would you define trials?
- What kinds of trials do you think the believing Jews of that day were facing?
- What can you learn from the use of the word "various"?
- What is the natural reaction to trials?
- How are believers supposed to react? Why are we to react like this?
- What is the purpose of trials? What are two possible reactions to trials?
- How do these test our faith?
- How does this produce endurance?
- How does endurance bring us to maturity and make us complete?
- What might be the difference between the faith/character of a believer never exposed to trials (if there were such a person) and a believer who had faced many trials and passed the test?
- Share an example of a trial you have faced. What did you learn from it?

## Cross-References

Matthew 5:10 - Blessed are those who are persecuted because of righteousness for theirs is the kingdom of heaven.

Acts 5:41 – The apostles left the Sanhedrin, rejoicing because they had been counted worthy of suffering disgrace for the Name.

1 Peter 1:6-7 – In all this you greatly rejoice, though now for a little while you may have had to suffer grief in all kinds of trials. These have come so that the proven genuineness of your faith—of greater worth than gold, which perishes even though refined by fire—may result in praise, glory and honor when Jesus Christ is revealed.

Romans 5:3-4 – Not only so, but we also glory in our sufferings, because we know that suffering produces perseverance; perseverance, character; and character, hope.

2 Corinthians 4:16-18 – Therefore we do not lose heart. Though outwardly we are wasting away, yet inwardly we are being renewed day by day. For our light and momentary troubles are achieving for us an eternal glory that far outweighs them all. So we fix our eyes not on what is seen, but on what is unseen, since what is seen is temporary, but what is unseen is eternal.

## Teaching Points

1. Trials are good for us and are sent by God - Trials are meant to test our faith. They give us a chance to prove our love for God through action. It is often easy to say we love God and to be faithful to Him when things are going very smoothly. But what about when things become difficult? These are the times that require faith and show our true character. It is during challenging periods that many people turn away from God. Instead, we need to view trials as a chance for us to grow. Though trials are not easy, they are meant for our good.

**Application:** Think about a trial that you are facing. Spend some time in prayer and thank God for the good He is bringing about in your life through that trial.

2. Consider it pure joy – This is a mindset that James encourages his readers to have. Trials are certainly not enjoyable. Yet here we are commanded to be joyful even amid trials. Why?

The reason is given in verse 3. Trials test our faith and develop perseverance. Though a person would not normally look at a trial and say, "I am so happy my health is poor," or "I am so happy that I lost my job," a person could look at these situations and say, "I know that God has my best interests at heart," or "I know that losing my job is an opportunity to rely on the Lord instead of my own understanding."

Thus, when we face trials, we should always try to look at what lessons God wants to teach us in the middle of them. It is also possible that as long as we don't learn the lessons, the trial will continue until we do learn them. For example, when I pray for patience, God might even answer this prayer by sending someone who tests my patience into my life. And this trial may continue until I have truly learned the lesson that God has for me.

My wife and I gave our first daughter the middle name Patience. We wanted her to be a patient person, and so we thought that giving her this name would be a good reminder to her. But it seems that God wanted to use her to develop our patience. Of all of our babies, she cried the most. She had serious colic. During the daytime, when we weren't holding her, she would cry almost all the time. This continued for many months. We realized that God wanted to use her to teach us patience.

Trials are like this. At the time, they are not enjoyable. But God uses them to teach us lessons and help us grow. We did learn to be more patient, and even years later, the lessons learned during those times stick with us and help us to endure other inconveniences joyfully.

**Application:** What are some practical ways you can have joy in the midst of a trial?

3. Whenever you face trials of **many** kinds – Trials come in all shapes and sizes. We are not only to have a good attitude in certain kinds of trials, such as the ones that are relatively easy or very short term. But we are to have joy even during challenging trials or trials that go on for a very long time.

Paul had a thorn in his flesh that he asked God to remove three times, but God did not remove it because His ways our higher than ours.

One of my close relatives has struggled with serious pain in her neck for many years. This trial seems to go on and on. It is extremely difficult to face chronic pain day after day, but she maintains a cheerful attitude and still does what she can to serve others. This is a great testimony to the rest of us.

**Application:** Is there someone you know that is facing a tough trial? What can you do to encourage them and support them during this time?

4. So that you may be mature and complete, not lacking anything – God does not take away trials from our lives because trials are beneficial for us. They raise us up to maturity.

Imagine a child who grows up in pampered surroundings. He gets everything he wants immediately. He never faces challenges because his parents step in and solve them for him. How will this child end up? He will grow up spoiled. Then when he leaves home, and a real trial hits, he will have no idea what to do. He might go off the deep end.

The last emperor of China was a man named Pu Yi. He had servants who did everything for him. They brushed his teeth and tied his shoes. Pu Yi lived an extremely spoiled existence. Partially because of this, he grew up selfish and sadistic, caring nothing for others. When Pu Yi became a man and faced trials, he had no moral character or backbone. The result was he betrayed his people and his country. A few trials growing up could have really helped him.

**Application:** The Lord wants to bring us up to maturity slowly and surely. Write down one trial that you are facing. Then write down one area you think God wants you to grow in light of this trial.

# III. Pray with faith (5-8)

## Discussion Questions

- How does wisdom connect to the issue of trials just discussed?
- Who/what is the source of wisdom?
- What other places do people often turn to for wisdom?
- What kind of wisdom will we get from these sources?
- What is God's attitude toward us and our prayers?
- What does the phrase "without reproach" mean here?
- Through what methods might God give us this wisdom?
- What condition do we need to fulfill?

- Explain the faith mentioned in verse 6. Faith in what? What exactly must we have faith in? What kind of doubts may this refer to?
- Does the answer of prayer then depend on your own faith level?
- Why is the term "double-minded" used in verse 8?
- Share an example of a time when you needed wisdom. What did you do?

## Cross-References

Proverbs 3:5-7 – Trust in the Lord with all your heart and lean not on your own understanding; in all your ways submit to him, and he will make your paths straight. Do not be wise in your own eyes; fear the Lord and shun evil.

John 15:7 - If you remain in me and my words remain in you, ask whatever you wish, and it will be done for you.

Hebrews 11:6 – And without faith it is impossible to please God, because anyone who comes to him must believe that he exists and that he rewards those who earnestly seek him.

Mark 11:24 – I tell you, you can pray for anything, and if you believe that you've received it, it will be yours.

Hebrews 10:23 – Let us hold unswervingly to the hope we profess, for he who promised is faithful.

## Teaching Points

1. If anyone lacks wisdom (5) – True wisdom comes from God and not from ourselves. The world offers the appearance of wisdom, but only when looking at things through temporal eyes. God wants us to succeed and to follow His will by making the right decision. Therefore, God will give us true wisdom from Himself when we ask Him to. The problem is sometimes we don't want it.

In fact, we all lack wisdom quite often. The first test is to see if we will admit it or not. A prideful person seldom prays because he thinks he can solve problems on his own and with his own logic. When we are humble, we realize that there are so many variables we don't understand and can't control. We will realize how little we actually know and be motivated to turn to the Lord in prayer.

God will give generously and without finding fault. This phrase, "without finding fault," is quite interesting. He seems to be saying that God won't blame you for your lack of knowledge.

A child may ask his parents for help with his homework, and that parent may blame the child for not knowing the answer already. Here we see that God will not do this. Instead, He welcomes our questions and requests. He wants us to ask Him for help rather than going it alone.

2. He must believe and not doubt –

- Do we really believe God can and will answer our prayers?
- Do we really believe He is listening?
- Do we really believe He is all-powerful and all-good?

These are questions we must ask and solve before we approach God in prayer. We should then pray confidently, knowing He hears every word we speak and will answer. His answer may not be exactly what we want or hope for, just as a parent does not always give his child the candy or ice cream he asks for, but His answer will be exactly what is good for us, exactly what we need.

This is not a magic formula for getting whatever you want in prayer. You cannot force God to do something against His will just by believing it. And in the end, we can only have this level of belief in things we are sure are God's will. From this verse, we can be sure it is God's will to give us wisdom. So, we can believe it completely and not doubt it. Then He will give it to us.

# IV. Be humble and content (9-11)

## Discussion Questions

- Explain the term "brother of humble circumstances."

- What does it mean "to glory in"?
- In what way is does a poor believer have a high position?
- In what way will the rich man be humiliated?
- Do these verses teach it is wrong to be rich? If not, what do they teach about riches?
- What do these verses tell us about the importance of earthly possessions?
- What can a poor person learn from this?
- How about a rich person?
- What can we learn about the meaning of life?

## Cross-References

Proverbs 19:1 – Better the poor whose walk is blameless than a fool whose lips are perverse.

Luke 1:52-53 – He has brought down rulers from their thrones but has lifted up the humble. He has filled the hungry with good things but has sent the rich away empty.

2 Corinthians 6:10 – Sorrowful, yet always rejoicing; poor, yet making many rich; having nothing, and yet possessing everything.

Matthew 5:3 – Blessed are the poor in spirit, for theirs is the kingdom of heaven.

Jeremiah 9:23-24 – This is what the Lord says: "Let not the wise boast of their wisdom or the strong boast of their strength or the rich boast of their riches, but let the one who boasts boast about this: that they have the understanding to know me, that I am the Lord, who exercises kindness, justice and righteousness on earth, for in these I delight," declares the Lord.

1 Timothy 6:17 – Command those who are rich in this present world not to be arrogant nor to put their hope in wealth, which is so uncertain, but to put their hope in God, who richly provides us with everything for our enjoyment.

1 Peter 1:24 - For, "All people are like grass, and all their glory is like the flowers of the field; the grass withers and the flowers fall,

**Teaching Points**

1. Verse 9 – Although a person's economic position may be poor, his position in Christ is high (Galatians 3:28). He may be physically deficient but spiritually rich. Those who are poor in this world should not focus on their lack of material things. Rather they should focus on their abundant spiritual blessings.

2. Verses 10-11 – The rich person should realize that, in the end, he is just like the poor person. His riches will fade away. His life itself will be as short as many of the poor people around him. His riches and materials cannot buy long life (or not eternal life, anyway). And yet this person, if he trusts in Christ, can also be spiritually rich and full of blessings.

**Application**: If you have little, don't focus on that, but set your mind on the things above. If you have much, don't focus on that either (though you should be thankful). Instead put your mind on things above and be thankful for your blessings in Christ.

# James 1:12-27

## Outline

I. Temptation is not from God (12-15)
II. God gives good gifts (16-17)
III. Set apart through the Word (18-27)

## I. Temptation is not from God (12-15)

### Discussion Questions

- How is a person blessed who perseveres under trial?
- How can you help others persevere in the midst of trials?
- How can you persevere during trials?
- What is the crown of life?
- Why do you think James includes this reminder about God and temptation here in the middle of his discussion on trials?
- What is the difference between trials and temptations?
- If temptation doesn't come from God, where does it come from?
- Why is it important to know the truth about the results of giving in to temptation?
- How does it help us to know that we ourselves are full of evil desires in our battle against temptation?
- So then, what steps can we take to conquer temptation in our lives?

### Cross-References

1 Peter 5:10 - And the God of all grace, who called you to his eternal glory in Christ, after you have suffered a little while, will himself restore you and make you strong, firm and steadfast.

1 Peter 1:7 - These have come so that the proven genuineness of your faith—of greater worth than gold, which perishes even though refined by fire—may result in praise, glory and honor when Jesus Christ is revealed.

1 Corinthians 10:13 - No temptation has overtaken you except what is common to mankind. And God is faithful; he will not let you be tempted beyond what you can bear. But when you are tempted, he will also provide a way out so that you can endure it.

Proverbs 4:23 - Above all else, guard your heart, for everything you do flows from it.

Mark 7:21-22 - For it is from within, out of a person's heart, that evil thoughts come—sexual immorality, theft, murder, adultery, greed, malice, deceit, lewdness, envy, slander, arrogance and folly.

## Teaching Points

1. Persevere under trials - All people will face trials, and believers will probably face even more than average. It is not a question of if but when. We can't usually control the trials that we face, but we can decide how we respond to them. Believers are supposed to persevere. We are supposed to bear up under it. It might be helpful to look at the opposite of perseverance to understand what that means.

The opposite of perseverance is "giving up." When believers (or professing believers) face trials, they could just give up. They might do so for a number of reasons. Maybe they grow to doubt God's goodness, His plan, or even His existence. Maybe they still believe in God, but their flesh wins and they give up because it is simply "too hard" and too painful to persevere. But if you give up, you won't win the prize.

1 Corinthians 9:24-27 - *Do you not know that in a race all the runners run, but only one gets the prize? Run in such a way as to get the prize. Everyone who competes in the games goes into strict training. They do it to get a crown that will not last, but we do it to get a crown that will last forever. Therefore I do not run like someone running aimlessly; I do not fight like a boxer beating the*

14

*air. No, I strike a blow to my body and make it my slave so that after I have preached to others, I myself will not be disqualified for the prize.*

Perseverance is hard work. Like an athlete, we need to discipline ourselves. Athletes do not always feel like getting up early and training. Neither do we always feel like praying or studying God's Word. Our emotions are up and down, but following God is a choice we make based on faith.

Perseverance does not mean perfection. Nobody is perfect, but a righteous person falls seven times and rises again (Proverbs 24:16). Saints that persevere will emerge from the trial victorious, having never lost the faith and having maintained a positive and grateful attitude towards the Lord.

Perseverance is a sign that the person's faith is genuine. Trials act as a sifter to sift out false believers from the true ones. Those who truly belong to the Lord will heed the warnings in the Bible and endure victoriously and receive the crown of life.

**Application:** When you are facing trials, it is important to get help from other believers and not isolate yourself. Tell a close brother or sister in the Lord what you are facing. Ask them to pray for you and support you. This is what the church is for.

2. What is this crown of life? - Athletes in ancient times received a wreath placed on their heads, denoting their victory. This tradition is likely the imagery James alludes to. The crown referred to here is probably symbolic. It represents the believer's ultimate reward, the prize that we strive for. That prize is eternal life. In fact, it is already guaranteed to those of us who believe. It has been promised, but we will finally receive it in full when we emerge victorious from this life of trials.

Consider for a moment the process of buying a house. I place a down payment on it, sign a contract, and it is "mine," but I still need to make monthly payments. If I give up, it will be revealed that the house doesn't really belong to me. However, after many years, if I finish all the payments, then the house is completely mine. The example is not perfect, but you can imagine that our response to trials is like making continued payments. It confirms our faith. But if we give up under trials, it is like a person who stops making payments and the house is repossessed (no, this doesn't mean we can lose our salvation, John 10:27-30).

3. Trials and temptations are different - James makes an important distinction between trials and temptations, as well as their source. He makes it clear that God is never responsible for tempting people. Temptation comes from evil, but God is pure and holy, not evil. It is essential we know that God is not the source of temptation.

Otherwise, we may excuse our sin by blaming God and saying, "God is tempting me." After all, if God is the one who tempts, then who are we to stand in His way? But of course, this way of thinking is wrong. God never condones sin. He is not the author of evil. And He never tempts anyone.

Satan may use a situation in your life to try to tempt you to give up. God could use the same situation to encourage you to persevere and therefore strengthen your faith.

4. Temptation spawns from our own flesh - Temptation is only effective because it interacts with our lustful flesh. God cannot be tempted. Why? Because He has no evil or evil desires. We are tempted every day because we are evil and have evil desires.

Some things might be a temptation for one person but not another because their desires are different. One person may not be tempted by alcohol and drugs but may be tempted by lustful thoughts and sex. Another person may face little temptation in the area of gluttony but great temptation in binge-watching television shows. We must be aware of our own weaknesses.

Why is it important for us to recognize our weaknesses?

1 Peter 5:8 - *Be sober-minded; be watchful. Your adversary the devil prowls around like a roaring lion, seeking someone to devour.*

Satan is like a lion and wants to devour you. Lions have little chance of catching wary prey. Their only opportunity is to sneak up on unsuspecting victims and pounce before they are noticed.

To avoid this fate, we must humbly realize our own fleshly weaknesses so that we can protect against them. If we are prideful, then we will fall.

What steps can we take to protect ourselves against ourselves?

Here are a few ways:

- Fellowship. Surround yourselves with other believers who can keep you accountable.
- Get an accountability partner. If you know you are tempted in one area (for example, porn), ask a brother to check up on you from time to time and ask the tough questions.
- Avoid places or things we know will tempt us. One famous definition of insanity is repeating the same thing over and over and hoping for a different result. Break the cycle. Try something different.
- Set standards for ourselves of things we will or won't do to make clear lines. For example, decide ahead of time that you will not be together with your girlfriend late at night in a private place to reduce temptation.
- Pray immediately when we face a temptation. Make a habit to just say a simple "help me" to God in the moment of temptation.
- Fill our minds with the Bible. If you memorize Scripture, it will come to mind to protect and convict you.

What God says through James about temptation and the steps of it are very different from what Satan says. Satan might call temptation an opportunity for pleasure.

He might say, "Each person can enjoy himself fully when he puts off the old-fashioned traditions and narrow-minded bigotry. He can engulf himself in pleasure if he just is open-minded enough to think freely and be independent of external restraints. The pleasure will be enhanced when you fully let go. The fun gives birth to pleasure, which gives birth to continuing bliss. When it is complete, you will be the happiest person alive." The father of lies always promises more than he can deliver.

But God says that temptation realized brings about sin and that sin brings about death (Romans 6:23.) You can see the two opposing views in Genesis where God said they would die if they ate the fruit, and Satan said, "You surely will not die."

Who was right? God was. They died. And He still is right today.

We need to understand the consequences of sin. Sin brings about misery, guilt, despair, bitterness, self-loathing, pain, and death. It looks tasty on the hook but tastes sour in your mouth. Believe God, and don't fall for Satan's trap.

**Application:** Consider one area where you are often tempted. Make an action plan to reduce temptation in this area. Find a brother or sister, show them your action plan, and ask them to keep you accountable.

# II. God gives good gifts (16-17)

## Discussion Questions

- Satan wants to tell us that God is keeping us from something good, but what is the truth?
- Is there anything good for us that God doesn't want us to have?
- How does recognizing the goodness of God's character help us in our fight against temptation?
- How does recognizing the goodness of God's character help you persevere under trials?
- What does it mean that the Father of lights has no "variation or shifting shadow"?
- Who took the initiative to save us?
- What does the phrase mean "first fruits among His creatures"?

## Cross-References

Matthew 7:11 - If you, then, though you are evil, know how to give good gifts to your children, how much more will your Father in heaven give good gifts to those who ask him!

Psalm 34:10 - The lions may grow weak and hungry, but those who seek the Lord lack no good thing.

Psalm 84:11 - For the Lord God is a sun and shield;
the Lord bestows favor and honor;
no good thing does he withhold from those whose walk is blameless.

## Teaching Points

1. When tempted, remember that God is good - In the middle of teaching on temptation, James interjects statements on God's goodness. Why? Knowing God's goodness is also a protection against sin.

When Satan first tempted Eve, he tried to make her doubt the goodness of God. He told her that God was keeping her from something good, something wonderful. According to Satan, eating the fruit would help her become like God. It was God's cruelty and selfishness which restricted her from something beneficial. She fell for it, and the world fell into sin.

The truth is that everything good comes from God. He has our good at heart. When God gives us commands and rules, they are to help us, not harm us. People who reject God's commands in pursuit of pleasure will find themselves farther and farther from joy.

Jeremiah 29:11 - *For I know the plans I have for you, declares the Lord, plans for welfare and not for evil, to give you a future and a hope.*

Just as a parent restricts his children from indulging in candy (which tastes good but has bad side effects), so God restricts us from things that will harm us. Trusting in God and His goodness protects against temptation's enticements.

Take, for example, the case of two salesmen. One of them is your good friend, who you know will tell the truth. You know he cares for you and truly wants to help you. The other one is a famous scam artist. But his product sounds outstanding, and he is a fluent speaker. Who will you believe? The wise person will believe the one who is trustworthy! And James is telling us that God is trustworthy.

**Application:** Think back on your life and evaluate if there was ever a time when you doubted God's goodness in His plans for you. Confess to Him now and reaffirm your faith that He indeed wants what is best for you.

# III. Set apart through the Word (18-27)

## Discussion Questions

- Why should we be quick to hear and slow to speak? How can this keep us from sin?
- How does the "anger of man" differ from God's anger?
- In what way does it require humility to receive the Word?
- How does a person who is a hearer only delude himself?
- How is the Bible like a mirror?
- How might a hearer react to a sermon?
- How might a doer react to a sermon?
- Are you a hearer or a doer?
- What are some practical ways you can become a better doer?
- Why does looking out for orphans and widows portray pure religion?

## Cross-References

Proverbs 10:19 - Sin is not ended by multiplying words, but the prudent hold their tongues.

Proverbs 16:32 - Better a patient person than a warrior, one with self-control than one who takes a city.

Ephesians 4:26 - In your anger do not sin: Do not let the sun go down while you are still angry.

Colossians 3:9-10 - Do not lie to each other, since you have taken off your old self with its practices and have put on the new self, which is being renewed in knowledge in the image of its Creator.

Romans 2:13 - For it is not those who hear the law who are righteous in God's sight, but it is those who obey the law who will be declared righteous.

Psalm 39:1 - I said, "I will watch my ways and keep my tongue from sin; I will put a muzzle on my mouth while in the presence of the wicked."

Luke 6:45 - A good man brings good things out of the good stored up in his heart, and an evil man brings evil things out of the evil stored up in his heart. For the mouth speaks what the heart is full of.

## Teaching Points

1. We humble ourselves by listening to others - Christians are to be humble like Christ was. Part of humility is not thinking too highly of ourselves or our opinions. We should not think we are better than others. A prideful person is "quick to speak." He loves the sound of his own voice. Such a person will often jump into conversations to share his wealth of knowledge even when not asked. In his pride, he will talk over others by being louder and more persistent. In an argument, instead of listening while the other is talking, he will spend that time forming his next point. These types of people are not fun to be around. Don't be that person.

Instead, we must be ready to listen to others' ideas. When they instruct us, we need to be willing to listen to their counsel.

Proverbs 12:15 - *The way of a fool is right in his own eyes, but a wise man listens to advice.*

Proverbs 18:2 - *A fool takes no pleasure in understanding, but only in expressing his opinion.*

Proverbs talks a lot about wise men and foolish men. Wise men listen to others, while foolish men just want to share their opinion and show everyone how much they know. We must be teachable.

It is often said that God created us with two ears but only one mouth for a reason, and it makes sense. There is still a time and a place for talking, teaching, and sharing our opinions. But we should be slow to speak.

This means we should take the time to think over what we say carefully. Do not rush to lecture others because once you say it, you can't take it back. Before you speak, ask yourself several basic questions. Is it edifying? Is it true? Is it helpful? Is it kind? Are we saying it in love? Is it gentle?

**Application:** List out three practical ways you will guard yourself from being quick to speak this week.

2. The anger of man is contrasted with the righteousness of God -

James 1:20 - *For the anger of man does not produce the righteousness of God.*

Did you know that believers are commanded to "be angry" (Ephesians 5:26)? There are two kinds of anger: righteous anger and selfish anger. Selfish anger is far more common. Here are a few examples of selfish anger:

- Getting upset when someone cuts in line
- Honking in anger at others' rude driving habits
- Complaining about our boss behind his back
- Yelling out our spouse during an argument
- Retaliating verbally to those who insult us

Selfish anger is always sin, 100% of the time. You cannot be angry about the above or like situations and not sin. A person who has selfish anger is focused on themselves.

They have been wronged, insulted, or mistreated, and so they react. People who get angry for these things are primarily concerned with their own rights and feelings.

Righteous anger is different. A person who has righteous anger is upset when God's moral code is violated. Generally, his anger is stirred up when the weak and defenseless are mistreated. Here are some examples:

- Jesus was angry at the people doing business in the temple
- Citizens were angry at the Nazis for killing Jews
- Being incensed at the treatment of orphans
- Being angry at the perpetrators of human trafficking
- Being angry that abortion is tolerated, legalized, and promoted
- Standing up for a woman who is being domestically abused

A person who has righteous anger is concerned with others. A person with righteous anger is concerned with God's glory and God's law, like Jesus was when He cleansed the temple. From this standpoint, God wants us to be angry. The opposite of righteous anger is apathy. Many people suffer from apathy toward others. Those who are apathetic are preoccupied with themselves and too busy to think or care about helping the weak and innocent.

I read a story about a little girl who was hit by a vehicle. Lying on the side of the road injured, bleeding, and crying, person after person passed her by. Later, camera footage showed fourteen people walking by her. Many were looking at their phones or turning away. They were apathetic. Such a scene should make us angry. Angry at the driver who left. Angry at a society that is too busy surfing social media to reach out and help someone in need.

Man's anger does not achieve the righteousness God desires. But this does not mean we should never be angry. Righteous anger can motivate us to take action and make a difference in society and in others' lives.

**Application**: What kind of things make you angry? Give an example of an area you have shown selfish anger. Give an example of an area you have righteous anger.

3. Receive with meekness the implanted word (21) - Here, we once again learn the importance of humility. It takes humility to submit ourselves to God's Word. We need to realize that we don't know everything.

Do not be offended if someone comes to you and shares with you from the Bible, even if he tells you what you are doing is wrong and you need to repent. God is talking through His Word and just using a person as a messenger.

4. Be a doer and not a hearer only - I think this is one of the most important principles in the Bible--being a doer, not only a hearer. We should study and obey! Christianity is not about head knowledge. It is not about how many doctrines you know, how many verses you have memorized, how well you know Greek or Hebrew, or how many times you have read the Bible.

Christianity is all about putting the principles we learn in the Bible into practice. It is worse than worthless for us if we learn the Bible front to back and back to front but don't do what it says. All that will do is cause God to judge us even more strictly because we have a higher level of knowledge.

You can go to a thousand Bible studies and listen to ten thousand sermons, but it is worse than worthless if you don't decide to follow them. No one else can make you do what God says. That is your own decision.

**Application:** Consider this an application to make an application. When you go to church, do you normally apply what you learn in the sermon? When you go to Bible study, do you make real life changes? Here is a simple way to open yourself up to be changed by what you are learning. Each time you study God's Word, write down one simple way you will obey what you have learned. For more on making SMART applications, visit our article, "What Should I Obey?"

5. Bridling the tongue - What comes out of the mouth often indicates what is going on in a person's heart. If a person has a loose and evil tongue, the likelihood is that their heart is like that

24

too. Jesus said that out of the abundance of the heart, the mouth speaks. Religion is worthless if it doesn't bring righteous action. For more on the tongue, see our study in James 4.

6. Pure religion is looking after orphans and widows - Why does James describe pure religion as reaching out to orphans and widows? First, we know that love is the mark of believers. True love is love shown with no thought of return. We know that it is easy to "love" those who love us. People often "love" others when they think they can get something from them. Love in marriage is often like that. They vow to love each other until death does them part...or until the other side stops satisfying them.

That is not true love. However, love shown to orphans and widows typically cannot be repaid. You will not gain anything from a worldly standpoint by showing compassion and mercy to this group of people. And that is why God is so pleased with this expression of love (Matthew 25:34-40).

The next thing James mentions is holy living. The Jews thought true religion was ceremonies, washing of hands, and external rituals. But it's not. True religion is inward holiness that will be expressed outwardly in our actions.

**Application:** What will you obey this week from what you have learned in the passage today?

# James 2:1-13

## Outline

I. Show no partiality (1-4)
II. Do not honor the rich above the poor (5-7)
III. Fulfill the law by loving others (8-13)

## I. Show no partiality (1-4)

### Discussion Questions

- What does it mean to show favoritism?
- Is favoritism common in your society?
- Why do people normally show favoritism?
- What are some of the motivations behind favoritism?
- Is favoritism common in the church?
- In what ways might believers show favoritism today in the church?
- How about outside of the church?

### Cross-References

1 Corinthians 12:12-14 - Just as a body, though one, has many parts, but all its many parts form one body, so it is with Christ. For we were all baptized by one Spirit so as to form one body—whether Jews or Gentiles, slave or free—and we were all given the one Spirit to drink. Even so the body is not made up of one part but of many.

1 Samuel 16:7 - But the Lord said to Samuel, "Do not consider his appearance or his height, for I have rejected him. The Lord does not look at the things people look at. People look at the outward appearance, but the Lord looks at the heart."

John 7:24 - Stop judging by mere appearances, but instead judge correctly.

## Teaching Points

1. Show no partiality - Favoritism is prevalent in the world. The way James describes this issue means to elevate or exalt a person based only on something external, such as appearance (skin color or race), wealth, gender, social status, or position. Nations have shown favoritism by not allowing certain minorities to vote or oppressing segments of the population in other ways.

The slave trade was a disgusting demeaning of Africans, whereby they were treated worse than animals. Even after African Americans won the right to vote according to the law, actually voting was very difficult for them in many areas of the US. Women also couldn't vote for an extended portion of American history. Some nations still only allow the rich to vote.

In South Africa, Apartheid kept a division between the white ruling class and the black class for decades. Some countries' majority have committed genocide against tens of thousands only because of a difference in race. In Rwanda in 1994, 800,000 minority people were brutally murdered in three months because of partiality. And Hitler massacred around seven million Jews under Nazi Germany, in addition to countless mentally disabled, elderly, and those who were not of his supposed Master Aryan race.

Favoritism is not limited to one race or group of people. It is a sin that any person, race, and country can struggle with. Moreover, it is ugly wherever it rears its head.

On a personal level, favoritism is just as heinous. It causes neighbors to turn against neighbors and the rich to abuse the poor. Favoritism can stir up hatred and bitterness.

Partiality also frequently pops up in religion. During the time of Jesus, the Jews were extremely prejudiced. They looked down on women, Samaritans, tax collectors, the uneducated, and all outsiders; basically everyone but educated Jewish males.

In the Middle Ages, the Catholic Church launched over ten crusades, most for the sole purpose of killing the heathen. And Muslims also fought many wars against the infidel to expand their territory.

Partiality is not only a thing from the ancient past. Today I have heard stories of people going to church and those in the congregation looking down on them and making them feel so uncomfortable (maybe because of their past sins, clothing, or other reasons) that they never returned.

In this passage, we are commanded to show no partiality. We are to love all people with the love of Christ regardless of skin color, sinful lifestyle, or economic position.

Galatians 3:28 - *There is neither Jew nor Greek, there is neither slave nor free, there is no male and female, for you are all one in Christ Jesus.*

2. What is the cause of favoritism? - I think there are several root causes.

A. Pride - Sometimes pride in our own education, knowledge level, or maturity causes us to look down on others who haven't achieved the same level we think we have.

B. External focused - Often we show favoritism because we are focused on man instead of God. We don't want others to look at us and say, "Oh, look who he is hanging out with." We are worried that spending time with a certain group or person will draw negative attention from others. Peter faced this issue when he stopped eating with the Gentiles in fear of the Jews (Galatians 2:11-13).

C. Desire for praise - We do something kind for some people because we want them to notice and return the favor, which is what James describes in this passage. If a person is rich or has a high position, they can do a lot for us, whereas if they are poor, they can't. If they are a pastor or esteemed church member, they will recognize our service and think highly of us. Basically, we show favoritism by being nice to particular people to win brownie points. Although these good deeds to curry favor may look good on the outside, God sees our hearts. We should please God rather than man.

**Application:** The problem for us is when favoritism starts to creep into our own lives and attitudes. Think about how favoritism may start to influence your thinking and actions. Share one or two times you might have been tempted to show partiality. What was the root cause? Why were you tempted? How will you improve in this area?

4. James' example of honoring the rich in church (2-4) - The believers James wrote to fell into the sin of favoritism by treating the rich differently than the poor. They gave the best seats in the church to the rich, while the poor were afterthoughts.

How might we fall into the trap of showing favoritism in church?

- Hanging out with the same group and ignoring others.
- Giving special recognition or plaques to those who make large donations.
- Currying favor with rich people who can give a larger tithe.
- Not paying attention to newcomers.
- Not being helpful to certain people whom we have a low opinion of.
- Being rude to a person because we think their motives are not pure.

**Application:** Train yourself out of favoritism. This week at church, instead of going straight to your regular group of friends to chat, find someone new whom you may not generally talk with. Reach out to them and be friendly. Invite them to lunch or your house.

5. Our ultimate example is Christ - Jesus was sent to die for the sins of the world, not just for one group of people. God created all people in His image. He values each one, poor or rich, healthy or sick, high or low IQ. Jesus gave His life for the people of the world. It is in this fundamental truth that the individual value of all people rests. Since Christ does not show partiality, we must not either.

If Christ, the Almighty Creator, was not too good to or above showing love and compassion to the lowest of groups, how about us? Obviously, we are not either.

Self-righteousness and pride make us think we are better than others or make us want to flatter rich people to get something in return. God is just, fair, and objective. This is a fundamental attribute of His, and we should strive to follow the perfect example of Christ. His ministry was primarily directed to the poor people and sinners of the earth, not Pharisees or important leaders. The poor are more receptive to the gospel, and we should emulate Christ's compassion for them.

# II. Do not honor the rich above the poor (5-7)

## Discussion Questions

- Does God show favoritism?
- What does verse 5 teach us about God's character?
- In what ways did Jesus give us an example of not showing favoritism? (Choice of lineage, birthplace, ministering to Samaria, Galilee, poor, sinful, and sick)
- How can we follow God's example of impartiality in our daily lives?
- What is James' point in verses 6-7?
- Since the rich can be cruel, should we show special attention to the poor people?
- Why or why not?

## Cross-References

Isaiah 1:17 - Learn to do right; seek justice. Defend the oppressed. Take up the cause of the fatherless; plead the case of the widow.

Matthew 9:10-13 - While Jesus was having dinner at Matthew's house, many tax collectors and sinners came and ate with him and his disciples. When the Pharisees saw this, they asked his disciples, "Why does your teacher eat with tax collectors and sinners?" On hearing this, Jesus said, "It is not the healthy who need a doctor, but the sick. But go and learn what this means: 'I desire mercy, not sacrifice.' For I have not come to call the righteous, but sinners."

## Teaching Points

1. Do not favor the rich - James points out how illogical it is to strive so hard to please rich people while neglecting the poor. The poor were often the ones who were saved by God and belonged to God's family, while the rich often mistreated believers and mocked their faith.

Many poor people are among the happiest in the world and have strong faith in God. Christ largely ministered to the poor people of the world. But it did not take long for Jesus' focus on reaching the poor to be forgotten.

The saints' partiality was motivated by a worldly way of thinking, but even with a worldly way of thinking, it was ridiculous for them to endeavor so hard to please this group who mistreated them. Why focus most of your energy on satisfying the rich person who will likely reject you and the word you teach?

Notice that James is not teaching a kind of reverse discrimination to discriminate against the rich.

Exodus 23:3 - *And do not show favoritism to a poor person in a lawsuit.*

God offers salvation to both the rich and the poor. But because of the pride of their heart, it tends to be less common for the rich to accept it. We must show love to all of our neighbors, poor or rich. James uses this as an example because most tend to try to please the rich. If it were the opposite, he would have used an opposite example.

# III. Fulfill the law by loving others (8-13)

## Discussion Questions

- What is Scripture's royal law?
- Why is this called the royal law?
- How serious is showing partiality?
- In what way does failing the law at just one point make us guilty of breaking all of it?
- Since we have all broken at least one law, what hope do we have?
- When we are tempted to show partiality, what should we remember from verse 12?
- What is the law of liberty? Is this the same law as referred to in verse 10?
- If a person has no mercy towards others, what does this show about his heart?
- How are showing mercy and being impartial linked?
- Who is a person in your life that you need to show more love to? How will you do this?

## Cross-References

2 Timothy 3:2 - People will be lovers of themselves, lovers of money, boastful, proud, abusive, disobedient to their parents, ungrateful, unholy.

Deuteronomy 1:17 - Do not show partiality in judging; hear both small and great alike. Do not be afraid of anyone, for judgment belongs to God. Bring me any case too hard for you, and I will hear it.

Deuteronomy 16:19 - Do not pervert justice or show partiality. Do not accept a bribe, for a bribe blinds the eyes of the wise and twists the words of the innocent.

Galatians 5:1 - It is for freedom that Christ has set us free. Stand firm, then, and do not let yourselves be burdened again by a yoke of slavery.

# Teaching Points

1. Fulfill the royal law - The word law is used in each verse from 9-12. The law of God has been against favoritism from the time of the Old Testament. One example of loving your neighbor is to treat him fairly, regardless of his position in society. Of course, there are many applications of this royal law.

Jesus said that the most important commands in Scripture are to love God with your heart, soul, and mind and to love your neighbor as yourself. In every situation, when we consider what action God wants us to do, we should ask ourselves, "What is the loving thing to do?"

- Should you scold your wife or not: "What is the loving thing to do?"
- Should you yell at your child or not: "What is the loving thing to do?" Sometimes it might be loving to yell at your child, like if they are about to run in front of a car, but generally it is not.
- Should you visit your friend in the hospital or take a nap: "What is the loving thing to do?"
- So many problems you face can be solved by asking two questions, "Is this loving God?" and "Is this loving my neighbor?" If you learn to ask these two questions of yourselves regularly, it will be a successful study.

2. What does it mean that the person who stumbles in one point becomes guilty of all? -

First, what does it not mean? It clearly doesn't mean that if you broke one law, you actually broke every single law. Technically you can murder without committing adultery and vice-versa.

But the point is, no matter which law you broke, even the smallest one, you are a lawbreaker and are guilty. Regardless which of God's laws we have broken, we are transgressors. We are guilty in His sight. He doesn't divide commands and say, "Well, you've only broken 27% of the commandments, so you are 73% good."

It doesn't work like that. If we have broken even 1% of His commandments, we are a criminal, a transgressor, guilty, and deserving of His judgment. This is made clear when you see that the summary of the law is to love God and love your neighbor. If you disobey this by showing partiality, you have disobeyed the law to love your neighbor and therefore have broken the entire law.

Why does James bring this up? I think his point is to stress the seriousness of partiality. Showing favoritism is serious. If you treat people differently because of appearance or status, then you are guilty in God's sight and deserve judgment.

So, if God's law is like this, what is our hope? How can anyone escape God's judgment? Obviously, our only hope is to trust in Jesus Christ, who can pay the penalty for us! He alone can save us from our sins.

3. What is the law of liberty - If you try to deserve salvation by obeying every law, you will make yourself a slave of it and can never fulfill all of it. But God's grace sets us free from judgment. The Pharisees tried to earn merit with God by rigidly following a set of rules. But their hearts were not transformed. And the burden was too great for any to bear.

The New Covenant sets us free from the Old Covenant law and encourages us to serve the Lord with our whole hearts, not to earn merit, but as a loving response to His love (1 John 4:19). God's commands are no longer seen as painful restrictions to freedom, but rather a means to the most joyous freedom, freedom of sin and a way to express our gratitude for Christ's sacrifice for us.

**Application:** Spend some time in prayer. Thank God that you are not required to follow a set of rules in order to earn His favor. Thank God He has shown grace by giving you salvation you did not deserve.

4. Judgement is without mercy to the one who has shown no mercy - From the parable of the unforgiving slave, we know that a true believer will, in turn, forgive and show mercy to others, while a false believer will not. If we have not forgiven others, God will not forgive us.

If we do forgive others, it is because God has forgiven us and enabled us to forgive them. This is directly connected to the idea of partiality. Mercy overlooks people's flaws, weaknesses, and external appearance to extend God's love to them.

**Application:** What is one thing you need to obey from today's passage?

# James 2:14-26

## Outline

I. Faith without works is dead (14-20)
II. The examples of Abraham and Rahab (21-26)

# I. Faith without works is dead (14-20)

### Discussion Questions

- Is faith without works of any use?
- What is your reaction when people need help?
- How can the phrase, "I will pray for you," sometimes be a cop out?
- How can you make sure that you do pray for people that you say you will pray for?
- What is the main point of verses 15-16?
- What does living faith look like?
- What kind of works might accompany living faith?
- What does dead faith look like? Is dead faith a real faith?
- What warning should we take from this?
- How can one show his faith without works? Is it possible?
- What does verse 19 tell us about real belief in God?
- Is it possible to believe in God and not be saved?
- What is the difference between saving faith and non-saving belief like the demons had?
- Why do the demons shudder?
- How can you better put your faith into practice?

### Cross-References

Ephesians 2:8-10 - For it is by grace you have been saved, through faith—and this is not from yourselves, it is the gift of God— not by works, so that no one can boast. For we are God's handiwork, created in Christ Jesus to do good works, which God prepared in advance for us to do.

Luke 3:11 - John answered, "Anyone who has two shirts should share with the one who has none, and anyone who has food should do the same."

Proverbs 3:27 - Do not withhold good from those to whom it is due, when it is in your power to act.

Luke 6:44-46 - Each tree is recognized by its own fruit. People do not pick figs from thorn bushes, or grapes from briers. A good man brings good things out of the good stored up in his heart, and an evil man brings evil things out of the evil stored up in his heart. For the mouth speaks what the heart is full of. "Why do you call me, 'Lord, Lord,' and do not do what I say?

**Teaching Points**

1. The question: Can faith with no works save you? - This question has been around a long time. Works and faith have often been at the center of debate in the church. What exactly is necessary for salvation?

Some groups have gone the legalistic route, trusting in their good works to save them, believing that by strict adherence to rules, they can earn favor with God. Others have said the mind is the most important, while physical actions aren't. Therefore, just believe, and you will be okay.

It's a fundamental issue and one that James covers in detail here. Keep in mind that James is a practical book, so it is natural that James will emphasize its practical side. Is faith without works of any use? Can that faith save him?

2. The illustration (15-16) - James gives an illustration to prove his main point (that faith without works is dead). The example is this:

A person in need comes to you for help. With smooth words, you bless the person and wish them well, sending them on their way. Judging only by your words, it would appear that you have great love, compassion, and mercy for this person. However, you do nothing tangible to help this person. They go away exactly the same as they came, in need. Your beautiful words did nothing to satisfy their need.

Thus, the rhetorical question: what use is that? The obvious answer--it is none.

It is hypocritical, and it would be even better to just truthfully say, "I won't help you. I don't want to help you." The implication is that words are not as important as actions. Empty words are useless.

Just as words without action do not help people, neither does professed faith in God by itself show that someone is truly saved.

**Application:** What is our reaction when people need help? Do we truly help them out or just cop-out by saying, "I will pray for you"? If we say we will pray for them, do we really pray for them? Actions are more important than words. Never say, "I will pray for you," unless you actually will pray for that person.

3. Faith without works is dead (17) - In verse 17, James answers his question and shows the point of his illustration. Verse 17 is James' thesis for this passage. It is simple. Faith without works is dead. A central theme of James' epistle is Christianity practically lived out in everyday life.

In Chapter 1, he showed that trials test true faith. Perseverance in trials is an indicator that a person's faith is real and they are truly saved. Thus, response to trials is test number one.

Test number two is works. The point is similar to the one at the end of Chapter 1 about hearing and doing. Knowing a lot of things is pointless unless that knowledge changes how you live.

**Questions for thought:**

• What does living faith look like?

- What kind of works might accompany living faith?
- What does dead faith look like?
- Is dead faith a real faith?
- What warning should we take from this?

Simply put, this means a person with real faith will live a changed life. A person who is genuinely saved will bear fruit. Jesus taught the same thing.

Matthew 7:17 - *So every good tree bears good fruit, but the bad tree bears bad fruit.*

There is a warning for us here in this passage. No one should rely on a past decision they made responding to an altar call or praying the salvation prayer. Many people will wrongly trust in a previous decision that did not change how they lived. Jesus warned against this.

Matthew 7:21 - *Not everyone who says to me, 'Lord, Lord,' will enter the kingdom of heaven, but the one who does the will of my Father who is in heaven.*

You should evaluate your own spiritual condition by examining your fruit. Are you zealous for the Lord? Does the fruit of the Spirit typify your life? Do you love sharing the gospel? Do you delight in studying God's Word and prayer? Do you sacrifice things in your own life in order to pursue God?

Those things are evidence that you are a good tree. On the other hand, things such as attending church, being baptized, joining the choir, praying a prayer, owning a Bible, or calling yourself a Christian are not very good indicators of salvation.

**Application:** Examine your own life. Are you changed after professing faith in Jesus? Ask God to reveal areas of your life that need surrendering to Him. Pray and commit yourself to making Christ Lord of those areas.

4. Show your faith by your works - Verse 18 shows us the proper perspective we should have on the faith/works issue. Instead of getting into an argument where one believer says he has great faith

and another believer focuses only on his own works, the believer should show out his faith BY his works. In fact, there is no other way we can show our faith except by works.

Faith, by nature, is invisible and intangible. That means it can't be seen or touched. You might say you have faith, but that is impossible for others to know unless you show it by works. How can you yourself even be sure that you have faith if you are not living it out?

Jeremiah 17:9 - *The heart is deceitful above all things, and desperately sick; who can understand it?*

Our hearts are sinful. It is easy to trick ourselves into thinking we are saved if we aren't by quoting doctrines like justification by faith and, once saved, always saved. James is giving us a tangible test to confirm if our faith is dead dogma or alive and breathing in our everyday life. Being truly saved will affect how we live.

5. Not all belief is saving faith (19) - There are some kinds of belief that don't save. The demons believe God. This is probably a reference to Deuteronomy 6:4, "Here O Israel, the Lord our God is One." Satan and demons have mostly orthodox doctrines. They know the Father, Son, and Spirit personally. They believe in the Holy Trinity of the Bible. That is, they believe in His existence and power. They certainly know God created the world. We know they believe in the judgment to come (Luke 8:31).

But they hate God with all their hearts and fight against Him with every breath even though they know He is real and the Judge. They fail in the second part of the Shema in Deuteronomy 6:5, which commands us to "love the Lord our God with all of our hearts, souls, and minds."

Demons believe God, but they do not submit to Him. Neither do they rest in Him. So although they believe God, they do not believe in God.

This verse shows us very clearly that head knowledge doesn't save. Even acceptance of the fact that God is true doesn't save. Having the right doctrines doesn't save.

Acts 16:31 - *And they said, "Believe in the Lord Jesus, and you will be saved.*

Believe in the Lord. One must place their faith in Jesus and submit to Him as Lord in order to be saved. Agreement with a list of facts about God is not enough.

# II. The examples of Abraham and Rahab (21-26)

### Discussion Questions

- Does verse 21 contradict with the rest of the teachings in the Bible of justification by faith alone?
- Is this passage teaching faith by works?
- Then how can we reconcile the Scriptural teaching of justification by faith with this passage?
- What is James' main point in this passage?
- Which came first, Rahab's faith or works?
- How do we know she had faith?
- Would her belief in the God of the Hebrews have saved her if she didn't act on it?

### Cross-References

John 15:8 - This is to my Father's glory, that you bear much fruit, showing yourselves to be my disciples.

Romans 5:1 - Therefore, since we have been justified by faith, we have peace with God through our Lord Jesus Christ.

Romans 4:1-4 - What then shall we say that Abraham, our forefather according to the flesh, discovered in this matter? If, in fact, Abraham was justified by works, he had something to boast about—but not before God. What does Scripture say? "Abraham believed God, and it was credited to him as righteousness." Now to the one who works, wages are not credited as a gift but as an obligation.

Galatians 5:6 - For in Christ Jesus neither circumcision nor uncircumcision has any value. The only thing that counts is faith expressing itself through love.

## Teaching Points

1. Abraham's faith was proven through his works (21-24) - In verses 21-24, James uses another case study to prove his point, this time focusing on Abraham. Interestingly, this is the very example used by Paul in Romans to teach the principle of justification by faith (Romans 4).

Also, Genesis 15:6 states explicitly that "Abraham believed God, and it was reckoned to him as righteousness."

Romans 3:28 - *For we hold that one is justified by faith apart from works of the law.*

Romans 5:1 - *Therefore, since we have been justified by faith, we have peace with God through our Lord Jesus Christ.*

James 2:24 - *You see that a person is justified by works and not by faith alone.*

At first glance, it appears that James may be contradicting Paul's teachings of justification by faith. How can we reconcile James' teaching with Paul's? Is he contradicting Paul?

We know that Scripture doesn't contradict itself, so there must be an answer. When working with tough to understand passages, it is better to interpret them in light of the clear passages. The passages teaching justification by faith through grace alone are many and scattered throughout Scripture, including the verses shared above.

James himself acknowledges that salvation is a gift from God in James 1:17-18, and he quotes Genesis 15:6, which says that *"Abraham believed God, and it was reckoned to him as righteousness."* So, it is clear that James does not believe in salvation by works, and this passage, as part of Scripture, cannot be teaching that.

So, what then is the point?

We know that James is a book stressing practical living and showing us some tests we can apply to see if we are genuinely saved. In this passage, James emphasizes the action that must come from genuine, living faith. Teachers emphasize different points when talking to different audiences. Some audiences need to be reminded more to have compassion. Some need to be reminded not to tolerate sin. Some need to be reminded to be bold. Some need to be reminded to be gentle.

Suppose you listened to two different teachers emphasizing two different sides of the issue. In that case, you might think they contradicted each other or were very different, when, in fact, they just focused on different aspects. There are two sides of the coin.

Paul was setting forth the doctrines of Christian faith. Doctrinally speaking, justification is by faith alone. James is setting forth the principles of daily living. In daily living, our salvation, which is by faith alone, is borne out by our good deeds.

Which came first, Abraham's faith or his offering of Isaac?

His faith came first. Abraham first demonstrated faith many years earlier by obeying God's call to "go to the country I will show you" (Genesis 12:1). Even when God commanded Abraham to sacrifice Isaac, he first left his place and traveled to the location to be used for sacrifice. From the beginning, he believed that God would raise up Isaac from the dead (Hebrews 11:19). His steadfast belief in God led him to obedience.

Doctrinally speaking, we are saved by faith alone.

Practically speaking, this faith must show itself through action, or it is dead.

2. Faith and works are necessary - Verse 22 makes it clear that James doesn't minimize faith, saying that "faith was working with

his works." What should we get out of this? Both are necessary. We need to have faith and works.

I think we should take this as a warning against having head knowledge without practicing it. Are you a person with all of your doctrines lined up and squared away? Do you take pride in being able to defend your beliefs? Doctrine is good. Knowledge is important. But our actions are the window to our hearts.

3. The example of Rahab - James uses Rahab as another example of faith in action. Her works proved that her faith was genuine.

Did she have faith or only works?

Joshua 2:9-11 - *I know that the Lord has given you the land. We have heard how the Lord dried up the water of the Red Sea for you when you came out of Egypt. The Lord your God, He is God in heaven above and on earth beneath.*

Here is Rahab's statement of faith. It undoubtedly shows that she believed God is the real God of heaven and earth.

Following this statement, her actions then proved that she meant what she said. She risked her life in order to save the lives of the spies. In essence, she betrayed her own country, people, and idols because of her faith in the true God.

James has said that "faith without works is dead." If Rahab said this statement of faith to the spies and then reported them to Jericho's authority, it would have proved that she was still devoted to her own idols. It would have confirmed that her faith in God was not genuine, certainly not strong enough to change her lifestyle or affect her choices.

James said that Rahab was "justified by works." These works proved to Israel that she was loyal to Jehovah. It was because of these works (saving the spies) that she and her family were saved.

Faith and works are two sides of the same coin. Without faith, Rahab would never have risked her life for strangers. And without her deeds of protection, her professed faith would have been empty. As James says in verse 26, "faith apart from works is dead."

There are many people in the world now who call themselves Christians. About 2.3 billion people identify as Christians. A very large percentage of these people have no real evidence of that faith shown by their actions.

Perhaps they have a wedding in church (and then later toss away their vows). Perhaps they go to church once or twice a year. Maybe they have a party and invite their friends to their child's christening. But a neutral party observing their lives would not find any evidence that their belief is changing how they live on a day-to-day basis. Thus, many churches are dead because the faith of their members is also dead.

**Application:** This is a stark warning of the need for personal examination. Your faith should change how you live. Write down two ways your faith has changed how you live on a day-to-day basis. Write down two more ways your faith needs to be reflected in your daily life.

# James 3:1-12

## Outline

I. Warnings about the tongue (1-2)
II. Examples illustrating the power of the tongue (3-6)
III. The tongue cannot be tamed by man (7-12)

# I. Warnings about the tongue (1-2)

### Discussion Questions

- Why is James encouraging fewer people to set their hearts on teaching?
- Aren't we commanded to teach others and pass on our faith?
- Why will a teacher incur stricter judgment?
- What do you think James means by "become teachers"?
- Does this mean you should not want to teach others about the Bible?
- If not, then what can we learn from this?
- Starting in verse 2, James begins discussing the evils of the tongue. In what way is this related to verse 1 on teachers?
- Explain the phrase, "If anyone does not stumble in what he says, he is a perfect man, able to bridle the whole body as well."
- Does this mean that we can really be perfect if we can control our tongue?

### Cross-References

John 13:15 - I have set you an example that you should do as I have done for you.

1 Corinthians 12:27-31 - Now you are the body of Christ, and each one of you is a part of it. And God has placed in the church first of all apostles, second prophets, third teachers, then miracles, then gifts of healing, of helping, of guidance, and of different kinds of tongues. Are all apostles? Are all prophets? Are all teachers? Do all work miracles? Do all have gifts of healing? Do all speak in tongues? Do all interpret? Now eagerly desire the greater gifts.

Hebrews 5:12 - In fact, though by this time you ought to be teachers, you need someone to teach you the elementary truths of God's word all over again. You need milk, not solid food!

## Teaching Points

1. Not many of you should become teachers - Teaching is a more prominent role than many others in the body. Here, "teachers" probably refers to those in an official capacity with a recognized teaching position in the church. These people are in the spotlight, and they have a lot of influence over others. Their words have the power to bring people to the truth or mislead them. Often, such teachers are admired and respected. This attention can lead to pride. It can also attract people who enjoy being in the limelight.

We should take verse 1 as a warning to prospective teachers to take their role seriously. It is not about the attention. A lot of responsibility comes with being a teacher. Your words can have a significant influence on others and can alter the course of their lives.

Hebrews 13:17 - *Obey your leaders and submit to them, for they are keeping watch over your souls, as those who will have to give an account. Let them do this with joy and not with groaning, for that would be of no advantage to you.*

Teachers will be held accountable for their actions. James says they will face a stricter judgment than the average person. Because they have told others what is right and wrong, they will have no excuse before God. They cannot claim ignorance because God may just play back a voice recording of them teaching others what they claim ignorance about. Having the official capacity of a teacher is serious, and one should consider his motives very carefully. A teacher should also be extra careful what he says so that he doesn't misguide people.

At the same time, God has given every believer a spiritual gift, and some have the gift of teaching. If someone has this gift, they should use it, but they should not use it loosely or haphazardly. Before speaking, they should prayerfully go over their words and ensure they align with Scripture.

Before you give advice to others, verify that it is grounded in Scripture. Before you offer your opinion, make sure it is grounded in Scripture. Before you teach on a difficult topic, ensure that you have studied it and measure your words carefully.

Also, we should not use this as an excuse to be silent and not share the gospel or encourage others to follow the Bible. The Great Commission still applies to all.

Whether you have the gift of teaching or not, each person should pass on the things he has learned about God to others.

Hebrews 5:12 - *For though by this time you ought to be teachers, you need someone to teach you again the basic principles of the oracles of God. You need milk, not solid food.*

Note what the verse says. The Hebrew believers should be teachers. Each person should grow past the baby stage, learn how to feed themselves, and then, in turn, give food to babies. In like manner, every believer should pass on what they learn to others.

But we should be careful about the words we say. We need to make sure that the gospel we share is the same one as the apostles shared and that the encouragement we give is from God's Word. If you speak God's Word, you can't go wrong.

It is perfectly OK to say, "I don't know," when someone asks you a difficult question about the Bible. You don't have to know every answer to start sharing.

**Application:** Do share testimonies and Scripture to encourage other believers. Do share the gospel. Don't be hasty to go on stage, claim a title, or share your opinion on matters you are not ready for.

2. We all stumble - Everyone stumbles with the tongue, but teachers even more so. Teachers speak and teach. That is what they do. Because they talk so much, they have more opportunities than average to stumble with their words. And incorrect words spoken by a teacher will have a greater negative impact than the average person since more people listen to them.

3. What does it mean that he "is a perfect man"? - There are two possible explanations for this. The first is that "perfect" truly means "perfect." That is, if a person is able to control his tongue completely, it is a sign of total self-control, and that person can control the rest of his body and be truly perfect.

However, we know from verse 8 that no person can actually control their tongue. So, the first explanation is that this is a hypothetical situation telling us that the tongue is the most difficult part of the body to control. "If" you controlled your tongue, you would be perfect. But you don't. So, you aren't.

The other possibility is that "perfect" means mature and shows that the spiritually mature can tame the tongue.

Whichever interpretation you favor, it means that taming the tongue is very difficult and we need God's help.

# II. Examples illustrating the power of the tongue (3-6)

### Discussion Questions

- What examples from nature does James give us?
- How do these relate to the tongue?
- Why do you think James has such a negative view of the tongue?

- How can our tongue defile our entire body?
- How does it set the course of our life on fire?
- Since the tongue has such capacity for evil, should we just cut it out?
- Would this solve the problem?
- What is the root of the problem?
- What is an example of sinful speech that you sometimes struggle with?
- What are some practical ways that you can reduce evil speech?
- What are some practical ways that you can use your words for good?

## Cross-References

Ephesians 5:4 - Nor should there be obscenity, foolish talk or coarse joking, which are out of place, but rather thanksgiving.

2 Timothy 2:14 - Keep reminding God's people of these things. Warn them before God against quarreling about words; it is of no value, and only ruins those who listen.

Proverbs 10:19 - Sin is not ended by multiplying words, but the prudent hold their tongues.

Psalms 39:1 - I said, "I will watch my ways and keep my tongue from sin; I will put a muzzle on my mouth while in the presence of the wicked."

Colossians 3:8-10 - But now you must also rid yourselves of all such things as these: anger, rage, malice, slander, and filthy language from your lips. Do not lie to each other, since you have taken off your old self with its practices and have put on the new self, which is being renewed in knowledge in the image of its Creator.

## Teaching Points

1. Illustrations on the tongue - James often uses illustrations from everyday life or nature to prove his points. We have seen illustrations about faith, works, and partiality in Chapter 2, and here, illustrations about the tongue. Maybe he learned this

technique of parables from Jesus, his half-brother. Illustrations are effective because they bring lofty and sometimes difficult-to-understand concepts down to our realm of experience and understanding.

Generally, parables or illustrations contain one important point.

**Application:** Illustrations are a beneficial teaching tool. For Bible study leaders, try to use illustrations often to help those in your group fully understand the text.

2. The illustration of the horse and bit and ship and rudder - Both of these illustrations have the same meaning. Horses and ships are hard to control. But it is possible to control them. A small tool (bit and rudder) can help you to steer these powerful objects. The bit and rudder are little parts of their respective whole but are extremely important if you want to control the whole. They are small but hold great influence.

In similar manner, the tongue is also little, but it too holds tremendous power. If you can control the tongue, you can control the body.

**Question for thought**: What are some practical ways to control your tongue?

3. The illustration of the fire and the forest - In verses 5-6, we see the amazing destructive capacity of the tongue. A fire starts off very small but can spread quickly and devour millions of acres before it burns out. Often, fires are started by careless people who smoke and don't put out their cigarettes or leave a few sparks at the bottom of a campfire. A little spark in the right conditions can lead to expansive wildfires that destroy life and property. Just a few seconds of care on the front side can save vast devastation later.

And once that fire starts spreading, even the coordinated effort of thousands of firefighters often can't stop it. The time to stop a wildfire is before it starts!

The tongue is the same. Words, once spoken, cannot be unsaid. Kids on playgrounds like to say, "Sticks and stones may break my bones, but words will never hurt me." But the saying cannot be further from the truth. Words can hurt. They do hurt. You surely can remember times when people have spoken hurtful things to you, and that hurt may still be there. Words can rip apart relationships, cause depression, and start wars.

King Solomon's son, Rehoboam, discovered the hard way the harm foolish words can do. After he became king, the eleven non-Judah tribes came to him to ask that their workload be lightened. The elders encouraged him to speak gently, knowing that a "gentle answer turns away wrath." But Rehoboam instead listened to hotheads. See what he says.

1 Kings 12:8, 14 - *But he abandoned the counsel that the old men gave him and took counsel with the young men who had grown up with him and stood before him. He spoke to them according to the counsel of the young men, saying, "My father made your yoke heavy, but I will add to your yoke. My father disciplined you with whips, but I will discipline you with scorpions."*

As a result, the other tribes revolted, and there was war for generations.

Another example of words spreading like wildfire is the crucifixion of Jesus, as many of the same people that shouted "Hosanna" days earlier shouted "Crucify Him" because of the poisonous whispers of the Pharisees.

A fire can damage in different ways. Not only does it burn, but smoke goes far beyond the actual fire, choking, stinging, and spreading an awful smell. Words can also extend far beyond what you expect and impact others, even in faraway places.

So, should we cut out our tongues (or just not speak) to keep from hurting others?

Jesus said that out of the abundance of the heart, the mouth speaks. Cutting out our tongues could, in fact, help us control what we say. We couldn't say anything. With our words, we couldn't slander, gossip, lie, boast, etc. But it would leave our hearts unchanged. We could then still use our body language, gestures, or writing to do those very things. Much can be communicated through a glare.

The root of the problem is our sinful heart. We are sinful people. The key is to let our hearts be regenerated, renewed, and cleaned, like David prayed to God to create in him a clean heart. If we don't have the desire to lie, we won't. If we don't want to harm people through slander, we won't. Yet we still must learn to control our tongues for two reasons:

Firstly, there are still remnants of our old nature left. Some wrong desires are still there. Temptations rise up. We need first to not say the wrong thing, then confess the thought to the Lord and move on. If you speak it out, the problem will often grow. One lie will bring another, which will bring two, and then three more. When you start to argue, it is tough to stop. The other person will likely respond in kind, and then you will respond in anger, and the issue will grow. The solution is to stop it at the beginning.

Secondly, our tongues are very fast. Sometimes they act before our mind can really evaluate what we are saying. This is often the case with jokes or ridiculing others. In this situation, we need to apply James 1:19 and be quick to listen and slow to speak.

**Application:** Share a time when you have hurt someone or been hurt by words. Share some methods that help you avoid negative speech.

4. The other side of the coin is to speak positive words - The solution to tongue problems is not to remain silent. Though the tongue is very powerful with the potential for great harm, it also has the potential for great good. That is why God gave us tongues!

Proverbs 25:11 - *A word fitly spoken is like apples of gold in a setting of silver.*

Without speaking, we cannot share the gospel. Without speaking, we cannot encourage others. Let us learn to use our words to pursue peace and build others up.

After two and a half tribes returned home to their side of the Jordan, the residents misunderstood a memorial altar they had built and thought they were rebelling against the Lord.

Gathering for war, they charged down there and angrily accused their brethren of rebellion.

Joshua 22:15 - *'What is this breach of faith that you have committed against the God of Israel in turning away this day from following the Lord by building yourselves an altar this day in rebellion against the Lord?"*

The spark is there. The two sides are at an intersection. War is moments from breaking out. A bit of pride, a bit of insolence, a bit of hasty speech, and a devastating war would be unavoidable.

But the Reubenites answered graciously and humbly, calmly communicating the reasons they built this memorial and reaffirming their faith in the Lord. Their cool heads and gentle words brought peace and restored the relationship (Joshua 22). On the other hand, if they had remained silent, the result would have been very different.

**Application:** Consider how to use your words to encourage others. This week intentionally speak edifying words to build others up each day. For example, you can aim to give at least three compliments to your spouse every day this week!

# III. The tongue cannot be tamed by man (7-12)

## Discussion Questions

- Why is the tongue so difficult to tame?
- What are some practical ways to tame your tongue?
- Why is the tongue so destructive?

- Give some examples from the Bible about the destructive power of the tongue.
- What are some ways you have hurt people with your speech?
- What does the fact that no one can tame the tongue tell us about the total depravity of man?
- Since no one can tame the tongue, what hope do we have?
- Besides destruction, what other potential does our tongue have?
- What does verse 9 tell us about our speech?

## Cross-References

Titus 2:8 - And soundness of speech that cannot be condemned, so that those who oppose you may be ashamed because they have nothing bad to say about us.

Proverbs 15:1-4 - A gentle answer turns away wrath, but a harsh word stirs up anger.
The tongue of the wise adorns knowledge, but the mouth of the fool gushes folly. The eyes of the Lord are everywhere, keeping watch on the wicked and the good. The soothing tongue is a tree of life, but a perverse tongue crushes the spirit.

1 Peter 4:11 - If anyone speaks, they should do so as one who speaks the very words of God. If anyone serves, they should do so with the strength God provides, so that in all things God may be praised through Jesus Christ. To him be the glory and the power for ever and ever. Amen.

Matthew 5:13 - You are the salt of the earth. But if the salt loses its saltiness, how can it be made salty again? It is no longer good for anything, except to be thrown out and trampled underfoot.

## Teaching Points

1. An illustration about wild beasts - James uses another example from nature, this time about wild beasts. His point is that although man can control and tame wild beasts, we cannot, of our own power, control the tongue. The tongue is more difficult to tame than a lion. Skilled trainers can train the lions or tigers to be tame

with much hard work. But no one can fully tame their own tongue without help from God.

2. No man can tame the tongue - We are sinful and depraved. Without God's help, we cannot hope to have victory or self-control in this area. But we do have hope. Our hope is in Christ. He gives us the strength to have victory (1 Cor 10:13), where the natural man can have none. A natural man may hope to suppress his tongue for a while, but like a lion that is not fully trained, it may spring up to attack at any time, surprising everyone around.

Some of my co-workers seem like nice people. Clean cut. They say kind things to one another and show care for people. But almost all of them, even the young ladies, curse. It was kind of surprising to me at the beginning to see these young, seemingly nice ladies suddenly curse in anger in the middle of the office. But it is quite common.

Outbursts are inevitable unless the heart has been regenerated by the Spirit. As believers, we can walk by the Spirit (Galatians 5:26). The fruit of the Spirit includes self-control. This is a winnable battle if we rely on God.

What steps can we take to win this battle?

A. Have a close relationship with God first. Jesus said that apart from Him, we can do nothing (John 15:5). Don't be fake or hypocritical. If you are trying to live the Christian life in your own strength, you will fail sooner or later.

B. Think before we speak. Don't be hasty to share your opinion. There is nothing the matter with talking, but don't find yourself always the one talking on and on.

C. If we have a temptation to sin with our words, pray immediately. It doesn't have to be long or complicated. Simply say, "God, I am angry. Help me."

D. Make a focused effort to be proactively using our tongues to glorify God and bless man. Train yourselves to speak positive words through practice. The more kind words that flow from your mouth, the easier they will come. But the more angry words flow from your mouth, the easier they will come.

3. Don't be a hypocrite (9-12) - These verses tell us that tongues reveal the hypocrisy in our hearts. If the heart is evil, sooner or later, in some way, a person's words will give it away. The tongue is too hard to control because it is so fast and seems to have a mind of its own.

Isaiah 29:13: *And the Lord said: "Because this people draw near with their mouth and honor me with their lips, while their hearts are far from me.*

This was another kind of hypocrisy. God doesn't want this kind of false lip service. Don't say it in worship songs if you don't mean it. It is worse to give false praise to God than none at all. How many people curse or belittle their spouses on the way to church and then stand up, smile, and sing loud praises to God once they arrive?

Yet the application for us is not to stop praising God; it is to stop using our tongues as weapons to hurt people. The solution is not to be hypocrites. We need to be honest and sincere. Our faith in God should touch every part of our lives. It should change our behavior.

Have integrity. Oil and vinegar don't mix. Next time you are about to enter an argument, mock others, scoff, ridicule, boast, lie, etc., think about Sundays when you tell God how much you love Him and when you worship Him with your words. Remember that it is hypocrisy for both blessings and curses to come out of the same mouth. We are to speak to one another in psalms, hymns, and spiritual songs.

**Application:** Spend some time evaluating your speech. Write down one or more areas where the Spirit has convicted you today and your speech has not honored God. Then spend some time in prayer. Confess your hurtful words to God. Ask Him to help you tame your tongue. If necessary, go apologize to anyone you have hurt with your speech. Commit to praying daily for your speech this week, and intentionally build up others.

# James 3:13-4:10

## Outline

I. Heavenly wisdom vs. worldly wisdom (3:13-18)
II. Worldly behavior (4:1-4)
III. Humble yourselves (5-10)

## I. Heavenly wisdom vs. worldly wisdom (3:13-18)

### Discussion Questions

- What key concept does James discuss in verses 13-18?
- How do you think an unbeliever would define "wisdom"?
- How would you define "wisdom" based on this passage?
- How would others know if you are wise since wisdom is an invisible character quality?
- Explain the phrase "gentleness of wisdom."
- Explain verse 14, specifically the phrase, "do not be arrogant and so lie against the truth."
- How can there be two different sets of wisdom? Can there be two almost opposite courses action that are both wise? Where does worldly wisdom come from? Is it really wisdom? If not, what is it?
- What are some of the key tenets of worldly wisdom?
- What are some of the key tenets of heavenly wisdom?
- What does this tell us about how understanding/knowledge/wisdom will affect our lives?
- In what way does verse 17 portray the characteristics of wisdom when it looks like it could just be a list of Christian virtues?

## Cross-References

1 Peter 2:12 - Live such good lives among the pagans that, though they accuse you of doing wrong, they may see your good deeds and glorify God on the day he visits us.

Ecclesiastes 1:2 - "Meaningless! Meaningless!" says the Teacher. "Utterly meaningless! Everything is meaningless."

Ecclesiastes 12:13-14 - Now all has been heard; here is the conclusion of the matter:
Fear God and keep his commandments, for this is the duty of all mankind. For God will bring every deed into judgment, including every hidden thing, whether it is good or evil.

Luke 22:25-26 - Jesus said to them, "The kings of the Gentiles lord it over them; and those who exercise authority over them call themselves Benefactors. But you are not to be like that. Instead, the greatest among you should be like the youngest, and the one who rules like the one who serves.

## Teaching Points

1. Review - James here continues his series of points on practical Christian living, focusing again on action instead of knowledge, doing instead of hearing. To look at it another way, he is speaking out against hypocrisy in the church. This hypocrisy comes in many forms, including:

• Professing faith in Christ but not persevering in trials
• Showing partiality towards certain people in the church
• Being a hearer but not a doer
• Saying one has religion but not looking after orphans and widows
• Saying one has religion but not controlling his tongue
• Blessing God and cursing man with the same mouth
• Professing faith but having no action to back it up

This passage contains two more areas to practically live out your faith:

- Considering yourself wise but not living it out
- Loving the world more than God

2. Who is wise and understanding among you? - James often teaches by asking rhetorical questions. Why? Asking rhetorical questions is a way to focus his message more directly on the recipients. It is intended to make people evaluate whether or not they are in this category. People are forced to consider his message instead of just thinking, "Oh, he is talking to someone else." Rhetorical questions are frequently used because James is a book that focuses on practical application, the living out of one's faith.

In this case, you need to ask yourself the question, "Do I consider myself wise and understanding?" If you answer "no," then we obviously need to work on becoming wiser. If you answer "yes," then he hits us with the phrase, "let him show by his behavior his deeds in the gentleness of wisdom." In other words, if you are really wise, live it out. And that is the theme in James' epistle, living out your faith.

Based on his teachings, it is safe to assume that James would have some choice words for people full of head knowledge but loose living. It seems his mission was to try to reconcile Christian living with Christian doctrine.

4. Earthly wisdom - Starting in verse 14, James begins describing earthly/worldly wisdom. He is giving a test by which we can measure if we are wise or not. We can look at our actions to see if we are living wisely.

So, what is worldly wisdom like?

Bitter jealousy and selfish ambition both indicate a competitive and combative spirit. You want what others have. You desire to push yourself forward no matter who you step on on the way. You look out for your own interests ahead of others. In conversations, you will probably boast about your worldly successes and discuss how to make more money and get a higher status. Earthly wisdom focuses on earthly riches.

I knew a lady who was very business savvy. She was especially clever with real estate. Buying and selling homes was how she made money. And every time I met her, she would talk about this, giving tips on how to make money through real estate. Most of her conversation was focused on profiting through real estate. She was earthly wise.

James 3:14 - *But if you have bitter jealousy and selfish ambition in your hearts, do not boast and be false to the truth.*

The end of verse 14 is saying that if you have this kind of attitude but think you are wise, you are being arrogant and lying against the truth. In other words, if you answered yes to the question, "Who among you is wise?" but have this kind of jealousy or ambition, then you are a liar and are not wise in God's eyes.

5. Two kinds of wisdom - The wisdom which says, "Look out for number one," is a selfish mentality that Satan has spread from the beginning. It can sound good or reasonable on the surface but is rotten to the core.

It goes back to the time of Cain and Abel. Abel pleased God. His sacrifice pleased God. But Cain's did not, and God was displeased. So, Cain was bitterly jealous of Abel and killed him.

There are two different sets of wisdom because the assumptions about life we base our decisions on differ. Evolutionists believe that there is no God. They will never be judged or held accountable for their decisions. After life, there is nothing more. Right and wrong are relative, they say, because there is no absolute standard; it is defined as what is good or bad for you or perhaps for society at large.

Now if you live with this set of assumptions, the wise course of action would be to pursue your own pleasure and your own selfish ambitions. Whatever makes you happy, do it.

But the Christian has a completely different foundation for living. We believe there is a God. We will be judged for how we live our lives. There is life after death. There is an absolute standard. Truth is absolute, not relative. Right is not about what is pleasant for us but what pleases God. Our actions are eternally significant. We are commanded to be unselfish and to put others first.

Different beliefs lead to radically different conclusions.

Wise for unbelievers is to do whatever brings them happiness. The wisest course of action possible, they think, is to please the one who sits on the throne (yourself) because there is no one else you will be accountable to in the end.

Wise for us, as believers, is to do whatever God tells us to do. The wisest course of action possible is to obey the one who sits on the throne and to whom we will be accountable for everything we do in our lives.

We need to understand the HUGE differences between heavenly wisdom and worldly wisdom when making choices.

## Application:

Do you want to make decisions with earthly, natural, demonic wisdom? Who is going to say "yes" to this question? Who is going to say, "Yes, I want to follow demons."

No one will say this, but the one who follows worldly wisdom is doing precisely that.

You must not simply follow the majority or go along with culture. We must instead critically check every decision we make and, most importantly, evaluate our lives to see if they align with our beliefs.

You want to go to college and get a degree. Ask yourself why. Ask yourself if God wants you to do that. Don't just do it because everyone else does.

You want to take the first promotion that is offered in your career. Ask yourself why? Ask yourself if God wants you to do that? Don't just do it because everyone else does.

You want to wait till late in life to get married? Ask yourself why. Ask yourself if God wants you to do that. Don't just do it because everyone else does.

You want to buy a house. Ask yourself why. Ask yourself if God wants you to do that. Don't just do it because everyone else does.

The list goes on and on. Culture is powerful. But worldly culture is against God's kingdom culture. It is earthly and, many times, demonic.

Exodus 23:2 - *You shall not fall in with the many to do evil.*

Culture is getting further and further from God. Powerful forces are at work that stir people up to reject and twist God's good designs. Satan is tricky. He will not walk up to you and say, "Hi, I am Satan. I have some demonic wisdom for you. Reject God's good standards and follow me!" No, he will be much more subtle. He will instead use positive-sounding buzzwords to cover the truly sinister teachings inside.

We need God's wisdom to discern the truth and stand up for it in a world growing ever more devoid of it.

If you only learn one thing from this passage on heavenly/worldly wisdom, I hope it is to be a Christian who lives out your beliefs in the world, not a Christian who lives like the world and also has your beliefs.

Ask God for wisdom, and He will give it to you (James 1:5).

6. More on the wisdom from above - Verse 17 looks like a list of Christian virtues. What does it have to do with wisdom? A Christian wisely living out his faith will be doing these things.

- Pure – Similar to without hypocrisy. Full of integrity, sincere. Proper motivation.
- Peaceable and gentle – The opposite of aggressive and assertive. Jesus is the prime example.
- Reasonable – Bible teacher John MacArthur says, "The original term described someone who was teachable, compliant, easily

persuaded, and who willingly submitted to military discipline or moral and legal standards. For believers, it defines obedience to God's standards."

- Full of mercy – James already discussed that those with true religion will look after orphans and widows in their distress.
- Good fruits – The faithful person will bear fruit.
- Unwavering – We won't give in when we face trials.
- Without hypocrisy – Being a hearer but not a doer, or blessing God and cursing man with the same mouth.

**Application:** In what area do you need more wisdom from above? How will you get that wisdom?

# II. Worldly behavior (4:1-4)

## Discussion Questions

- What is the main point of these verses?
- Why do you think James' often uses the rhetorical question/self-answer method to teach?
- Explain what James is referring to by "pleasures" or "hedonism."
- What group of people do you think James is describing in verses 1-4?
- If you had one word to describe them, what would it be?
- If he is talking to worldly people, unbelievers, then what can we, as believers, get from it?
- Explain the phrase "friendship with the world is hostility toward God."
- Why are friends of the world enemies of God?
- Does this mean we should hate the world?
- What is normally meant in the Bible by "world" or "worldly"?
- Do you love the world? Are you overly attached to it? Do you find yourself full of selfish ambition? Do you love the pleasures of the world?
- Can you think of some other verses in Scripture that talk about worldliness or the dangers of loving the world?

## Cross-References

1 John 3:22 - And receive from him anything we ask, because we keep his commands and do what pleases him.

1 John 5:14-15 - This is the confidence we have in approaching God: that if we ask anything according to his will, he hears us. And if we know that he hears us—whatever we ask—we know that we have what we asked of him.

Psalms 37:4-5 - Take delight in the Lord, and he will give you the desires of your heart. Commit your way to the Lord; trust in him and he will do this:

John 15:19 - If you belonged to the world, it would love you as its own. As it is, you do not belong to the world, but I have chosen you out of the world. That is why the world hates you.

## Teaching Points

1. James once again uses the question/answer method to teach - His questions generally highlight the main point he will focus on. James often brings up an issue with a question and then methodically answers it. The question implies that there were quarrels and conflicts among them. He was going to tell them why they had this problem. It was an external manifestation of an internal problem.

So, what was the internal problem they had?

2. The quarreled because they were worldly - We just looked at one type of person who is not living out his faith. He claimed to be wise but followed the world's wisdom.

In this passage, we see another type of person who is not living out his faith, one who claims to love God but actually loves the world. They are the apostate within the church, the goats that think they are sheep.

We've seen several tests to check if we are genuine believers, including:

- Test of trials (1:1-12)
- Pure religion (1:26-27)
- Faith/works (2:14-26)
- Heavenly vs. worldly wisdom (3:13-18)

And now James talks about a worldly lifestyle. The key problem is seen in verse 1. The source of all of these external problems is their pleasures. This doesn't refer to having fun but rather the issue of loving worldly pleasures instead of God.

The English word "hedonism" comes from the Greek word "hedone," which means pleasure. Some philosophers have used this word to depict their worldview on the meaning of life. Thus, a hedonist is a person that lives for pleasure.

Solomon tests this philosophy in Ecclesiastes 2:1-2:

*I said in my heart, "Come now, I will test you with pleasure; enjoy yourself." But behold, this also was vanity. I said of laughter, "It is mad," and of pleasure, "What use is it?"*

The love of pleasure is taking over many countries in the world. It is a large reason why the Roman Empire fell. In the beginning, the people were hard-working but once the nation became rich, they became lazy and wasted away their days. A similar phenomenon is happening in many Western countries now.

You have movie theaters, amusement parks, leisure spas, a TV in every home, personal computers with more TV on them, and handheld smartphones with even more entertainment options a click away. And these are just a few of the more ordinary forms of entertainment, and there are much worse.

The United States used to be very hard-working and goal driven. Now people are getting lazier and lazier the more they love entertainment. For unbelievers, this love of pleasure wages war in their bodies. They know they should work, but they cannot control their desires. These desires sometimes start off innocent but, left uncontrolled, they grow and can lead to fighting, quarreling, and even murder.

3. What is the proper outlet for our desires? The proper thing to do instead of trying to fill them ourselves is to go to God. Desire what He wants, and you will be fulfilled and joyful.

Psalm 37:4 - *Delight yourself in the LORD, and he will give you the desires of your heart.*

Pray for Him to give you the desires of your heart. An example would be a desire to get married. Instead of letting this desire grow uncontrolled and trying to fill it yourself by having a physical relationship outside of marriage or just marrying based on your own desire, you should take it to God. You say, "I have, but He didn't answer."

James says that maybe the problem is you asked with the wrong motives. Maybe you are approaching marriage by what you can get out of it rather than what you can give. Maybe you have a selfish mentality. Maybe your motivation is pressure from others or a financial motivation.

Or maybe you want money, so you ask God, and when He doesn't make you rich, you are surprised. Well, maybe you have the wrong motives. Perhaps you want to use the money for yourself rather than for God. You want to buy a bigger house, a large flat-screen TV, or go on a dream vacation. Some of our motivations are purely self-centered.

Of course, this does not mean that every time God does not answer our prayers, our motivations are at fault. But sometimes they are. We should be aware of that and learn to evaluate our hearts.

4. Friendship with the world is hostility towards God (4) - Loving the world is hostility towards God. A friend of the world is an enemy of God.

**Questions for thought and discussion**:

- Explain the phrase "friendship with the world is hostility toward God."
- Why are friends of the world enemies of God?
- Does this mean we should hate the world?
- What is normally meant in the Bible by "world" or "worldly"?
- What is an example of a worldly pleasure you love too much?

The world's system of thought is contrary to the Bible and righteous living. Some examples include such nuggets as "look out for number 1," "live and let live," "hakuna matata," and "no tomorrow." Materialism, superstition, loose morals, and selfishness are all examples of worldly living.

The world is ruled by Satan and manipulated by him. Therefore, friendship with the world is hostility towards God. We must choose one or the other.

1 John 2:15-17 - *Do not love the world or anything in the world. If anyone loves the world, love for the Father is not in them. For everything in the world—the lust of the flesh, the lust of the eyes, and the pride of life—comes not from the Father but from the world. The world and its desires pass away, but whoever does the will of God lives forever.*

# III. Humble yourselves (5-10)

## Discussion Questions

- In what way is God jealous?
- Isn't jealousy bad?
- What is the difference between good and bad jealousy?
- What does God's jealousy tell us about His character?
- What will God do to the proud people?
- Can you give some examples from the Bible of God humbling/judging the proud?
- Is there any middle ground that we can take on the whole world or heaven issue?
- What is the opposite of resisting?

- Is verse 8 directed towards believers? Why or why not?
- What is the main teaching in verses 8-10?
- What does it mean to "be miserable and mourn and weep"?
- Does this mean that since a believer is to hate the world and not give their lives to worldly pleasures, we will live in gloom and doom?
- In what way will God exalt us if we humble ourselves in His presence?

## Cross-References

2 Timothy 2:22 - Flee the evil desires of youth and pursue righteousness, faith, love and peace, along with those who call on the Lord out of a pure heart.

1 Peter 5:5-6 - In the same way, you who are younger, submit yourselves to your elders. All of you, clothe yourselves with humility toward one another, because, "God opposes the proud but shows favor to the humble." Humble yourselves, therefore, under God's mighty hand, that he may lift you up in due time.

## Teaching Points

1. He is jealous over our spirit -

Deuteronomy 4:24 - *For the Lord your God is a consuming fire, a jealous God.*

The Bible often states that God is a jealous God (Exodus 34:14, Exodus 20:5).

And yet people are also warned against the dangers of jealousy.

James 3:16 - *For where jealousy and selfish ambition exist, there will be disorder and every vile practice.*

Job 5:2 - *Surely resentment destroys the fool, and jealousy kills the simple.*

Is there a double standard? How can it be that God is jealous, and that is right, but people are not supposed to be jealous?

The answer is that there are different kinds of jealousy: righteous jealousy and unrighteous jealousy. They could also be described as rightful jealousy and unrightful jealousy.

Let us think of it this way. A husband and wife make marriage vows to one another. But later, another guy comes in and starts flirting with and spending time with the wife. He takes her to romantic dinners and gives her gifts. Should the husband feel jealous? Indeed, he should! If the husband is apathetic and says, "Meh, whatever," it is a sign that he does not love his wife.

The husband should zealously protect her honor. He should zealously commit himself to preserving the marriage. It is not only not good for him for his wife to be unfaithful. It is detrimental to her and her relationship with God. He should seek to protect her from sin. And any man that tries to woo his wife away from him is bad news and will destroy her.

In like manner, God is jealous when we pursue idols. An idol can be anything you set your heart on rather than God. God is our creator. He has the right to our affection. But at the same time, when we rebel against him and go astray, it is bad news for us. His jealousy is also others-centered in that He has our best interests at heart.

Would you want to be married to a spouse who doesn't care if you go out with others? Would you want to follow a God who doesn't care if you rebel against Him and face eternity in hell?

Righteous jealousy is a good thing because it protects purity and holiness.

On the other hand, not all jealousy is righteous. In Chapter 3, James describes jealousy and selfish ambition together. Unrighteous jealousy is basically the same as envy, which is selfishly desiring what does not belong to you. In the above example, if a man is jealous for another's wife, that is sinful jealousy.

2. God is opposed to the proud and gives grace to the humble - Since God opposes the proud but gives grace to the humble, we

should humble ourselves—simple logic. We don't want to find ourselves being opposed by God. That is the worst possible situation we could be in. God is the King, the Creator. We should humble ourselves under Him.

Psalms 2:2-4 - *The kings of the earth set themselves, and the rulers take counsel together, against the Lord and against his Anointed, saying, "Let us burst their bonds apart and cast away their cords from us." He who sits in the heavens laughs; the Lord holds them in derision.*

Proverbs 16:18 - *Pride goes before destruction, and a haughty spirit before a fall.*

God has established certain spiritual laws. One of these is that pride goes before the fall. If a person exalts themself, God will humble them. If a person humbles himself, God will exalt him.

And yet many do not learn this lesson. Many people are like the proud ones in Psalm 2:2-4. They refuse to submit themselves to God, wanting their own way. They think they know better than God. Seeking pleasure, they refuse to surrender to any authority that limits their freedom to indulge themselves.

Here are 10 marks of a prideful person:

- A lack of gratitude - Prideful people think they deserve what they get.
- Talking a lot - Prideful people have a lofty view of their own opinion so they often like to share it.
- Talking about themselves - Prideful people focus on themselves in conversation because they view themselves as more important than others. Therefore, they don't often ask questions of others.
- Anger - Pride and anger go hand in hand. The angry person is upset that his so-called rights are violated.
- Having a high view of gifts and skills - Prideful people have a very elevated opinion of themselves.
- Boasting - Prideful people find ways to exalt themselves in their speech.

- Belittling and criticizing others - One way to exalt themselves is to belittle others. By making others look small, they can feel big.
- Unteachable - Prideful people do not listen to instruction or reproof because they aren't wrong.
- Lack of asking for forgiveness - Prideful people seldom admit their mistakes.
- Lack of Biblical prayer - Prideful people rely on themselves, so they seldom pray.

Some of these marks come from the wonderful pamphlet "From Pride to Humility" by Stuart Scott.

What is true humility? Well, a humble person is exactly the opposite of the above list. A humble person looks at himself through God's eyes. It means we consider others better than ourselves (Philippians 2:3-4). Being humble is realizing that we are the created, that we are limited in knowledge and power, and that we are sinners in need of a Savior. It is not overvaluing ourselves or our own opinions.

At the same time, humility doesn't mean that we go around with a "woe is me" attitude or act pitifully all the time. Why? Because a humble person is not focused on himself at all. He is not thinking about himself. He is focused on others.

Neither does it mean that we always go around slumped over with bad posture and our eyes staring at the ground without any confidence. Humility doesn't mean weakness. Jesus was humble, but He was not at all weak.

**Application:** Look at the above list on pride. Identify which of these characteristics are manifested in your own life. Confess your pride to God and ask Him to help you grow in these areas. Then confess to anyone, starting with your family, whom you have acted pridefully toward.

3. Resist the devil and he will flee from you - Satan wants a weak target. He is not interested in going head-to-head with an emboldened saint who depends on God.

My children and I sometimes watch nature documentaries. We have watched one BBC series called "The Hunt." In this series, different predators are filmed going after their prey. You know what they all have in common? Predators always try to sneak up on their prey. They attack the young, the weak, the sick. Using the element of surprise is a common method of approach. And whenever possible, they attack from the back. You will seldom see a lion straight on attacking a giraffe, rhino, hippo, or elephant that is fully prepared.

So, James' advice for believers is simple, resist! Do not give in to temptation. You must identify those temptations which are the most enticing to you. Satan will attack in the areas you are weak. And then you must resist. Do not simply give in and say, "I always fall. There is no use." God will empower you if you turn to Him for help (1 Corinthians 10:13).

When temptation comes, flee. Quote Scripture. Pray. Call your accountability partner. Read the Bible. Sing a praise song. Tell somebody. If you develop a plan of resistance and call on God for help, then Satan will run.

1 John 4:4 - *Little children, you are from God and have overcome them, for he who is in you is greater than he who is in the world.*

Our victory is not in ourselves. We are little children. Our victory is in God!

4. Draw near to God in confession - A lack of confession is one of the marks of pride mentioned above. God is opposed to the proud. Therefore, He is opposed to the person who refuses to humble himself by confessing his sin.

Many of the mighty men and women of God in the Bible prayed amazing prayers of confession, even when they themselves were not the guiltiest (Daniel 9, Ezra 9). And God is always faithful to honor those prayers. He promises to forgive those who humbly come to Him and ask for it.

5. Mourn over sin - One of the marks of true confession is mourning over sin. Sin should cause grief. It is not to be ignored,

tolerated, or covered up. The strong emotion of sorrow motivates a person to genuinely repent and also make restitution where possible.

Ezra demonstrated this mourning in Ezra 9. When Ezra heard the news that the people sinned by intermarriage with idol worshipers, he ripped out his hair and collapsed on the ground. For an entire day, Ezra wept on the ground because of the sin, and finally, he prayed an outstanding prayer of confession.

Does your sin cause you grief? Too often, we take God's forgiveness for granted and mumble some quick "I am sorry" before continuing with our lives.

**Question for discussion**: What does real grief over sin look like?

6. Humble yourselves and He will exalt you - If we humble ourselves, God will exalt us. For some, this happens on the earth (Joseph, Daniel, David). For others, it may occur in heaven (Jonathan). Regardless, we know that God is watching us. We know that God is pleased if we humble ourselves and that sooner or later, He will reward us for that.

God is the only one who truly has the power to exalt people because He is the one with the highest position and authority to say who is exalted. For example, on this earth, people may exalt someone (such as Darwin or Marx or Steve Jobs). But God has the final say. And He may put those whom the world exalts to the highest place in the lowest, worst parts of hell.

Jesus blamed the Pharisees because they loved to exalt themselves. One way they did this was when they entered a banquet, they would immediately go to sit at the head table. Jesus told them that instead, they should sit at the lowest table, and then the waiter would come and ask them to move up, exalting them.

Jesus is our ultimate example. He humbled Himself by becoming obedient to the point of death on a cross, and therefore, God exalted Him. One day every knee will bow, and every tongue will confess Jesus as Lord (Philippians 2).

**Application:** Write down one way that you will humble yourself in the coming week.

# James 4:11-17

## Outline

I. Do not judge one another (11-12)
II. Remember, God is in control of your future (13-17)

# I. Do not judge one another (11-12)

## Discussion Questions

- What does it mean to speak against one another?
- Give some examples. What are some other Scriptures that talk about this?
- Then what does it mean to judge a brother?
- Does this mean we can't point out others' sins? Why or why not?
- What is the difference between the kind of speaking against/judging here and proper correction?
- What do you think a person's motivation might be in each situation?
- What does it mean that this person speaks against and judges the law?
- What law? How?
- What is the reminder in verse 12?
- So, what kind of attitude should we have about judging?
- A lot of sinning believers or unbelievers will say that Christians are judgmental and intolerant. They give Jesus' dealing with the adulteress women as an example that we should we be tolerant. Do they have a point?
- How do we balance confronting people with their sins and the fact that God is the judge?

## Cross-References

On slander:

Psalm 101:5 – Whoever slanders their neighbor in secret, I will put to silence;
whoever has haughty eyes and a proud heart, I will not tolerate.

Proverbs 10:18 – Whoever conceals hatred with lying lips and spreads slander is a fool.

Titus 3:2 – To slander no one, to be peaceable and considerate, and always to be gentle toward everyone.

Matthew 5:11 – Blessed are you when people insult you, persecute you and falsely say all kinds of evil against you because of me.

On judging:

John 7:24 – Stop judging by mere appearances, but instead judge correctly.

Romans 2:1-3 – You, therefore, have no excuse, you who pass judgment on someone else, for at whatever point you judge another, you are condemning yourself, because you who pass judgment do the same things. Now we know that God's judgment against those who do such things is based on truth. So when you, a mere human being, pass judgment on them and yet do the same things, do you think you will escape God's judgment?

## Teaching Points

1. Do not slander one another – God wants all believers to speak kind and edifying words about others.

Ephesians 4:29 - *Do not let any unwholesome talk come out of your mouths, but only what is helpful for building others up according to their needs, that it may benefit those who listen.*

The solution is not only not to bad-mouth other believers. The old saying, "If you don't have anything nice to say, don't say anything at all," is partially correct. But silence is not what God envisioned when He created our tongues. The solution is to intentionally think of positive words you can say to others. Words of complaint and frustration flow more naturally than words of appreciation and encouragement.

**Application**: You can set a goal for yourself to say a certain number of positive things about the people you live with each day or each week. Then you should consciously think of these kind things to say and find opportunities to say them. At the beginning, you may feel a bit awkward. If you keep doing it, you will find that it will come more and more naturally. And it will begin to heal your broken relationships.

2. When you judge the law you are not keeping it – No one is above the law. We should not pick and choose which Scriptures we will obey. Neither should we find excuses or loopholes. In many modern churches, certain teachings which are unpopular in culture today are glossed over, ignored, or outright changed. Sometimes they are deemed "cultural." Other times, they are interpreted as figurative. For example, many schools, even universities claiming to be Christian and conservative have abandoned the literal six-day creation account.

It is not a new inclination to pick and choose which Scriptures we believe in and follow. Thomas Jefferson did the same thing. Jefferson actually cut out sections of the Bible that he did not believe. Predominantly, these were miracles. Jefferson placed himself as judge over the Bible, picking the parts he agreed with to believe and rejecting the rest. That is not faith. That is not submission to God's law.

When a person does this, he sets himself up as the final authority, effectively acting as a law to himself. There is no purpose in even retaining a Bible or claiming to follow it with this attitude.

3. Who are you to judge your neighbor? – Should we judge others? You have probably heard people say something like, "The Bible says do not judge." But actually, the answer is not a simple "no" or "yes." We should look at these statements in context.

John 7:24 – *Stop judging by mere appearances, but instead judge correctly.*

In this verse, Jesus does not say to never judge others but says that we are to use righteous judgment.

But Matthew 7:1 says the following, "*Do not judge so that you will not be judged. For in the way you judge, you will be judged; and by your standard of measure, it will be measured to you.*"

Here Jesus warns that those who judge others will themselves be judged by the same standard, and He says, "Do not judge."

My belief is that we should not use our own opinions or convictions to judge others. For example, if I have decided that my teenage children should not watch an R-rated movie, rated so because of the violence inside, that is good and well. But I should not judge and look down on another family who allows them to do so. We should not use our own opinions to judge others in gray areas. If the Bible does not speak to a situation clearly, we should give others the freedom to make their own choices.

However, I believe I can and should stand firmly on the truth of God's Word to warn other believers who are clearly disobeying it.

1 Timothy 5:20 - *As for those who persist in sin, rebuke them in the presence of all, so that the rest may stand in fear.*

If someone disobeys a clear Biblical command, we can and should correct them. If you use Scripture to confront someone who has sinned, then you are not the one doing the judging. God is. God is the ultimate authority, and if you simply pass on His message to others unaltered, then you are not judging them.

For example, if you use Romans 3:23 to tell a friend that "all have sinned," then it is God doing the judgment and not you. We should not shy away from the truth of God's Word. When we use God's Word to correct people, we, in fact, are not the judges. He is since He wrote it.

**Application**: Do not hold other people to your own extra-biblical standards. But do use God's Word to challenge, motivate, correct, and rebuke when necessary.

# II. Remember, God is in control of your future (13-17)

## Discussion Questions

- What does it mean "come now"?
- Does verse 13 mean that making plans is evil?
- Is it that the plan of doing business and making profit is evil?
- What about if I say, "I will move to location X and spend one year there, start 5 Bible studies and train leaders, and then move on to another campus"?
- Is this better since my plan is a spiritual one?
- What is the point of verse 14?
- Do you know what will happen tomorrow? Who does?
- So, what is the problem with making plans on our own?
- What is the point of the comparison to a vapor?
- Is it enough if I say verse 13 and then add on a "if the Lord wills"? Are those four words the point?
- What is the right decision/planning process (seek God's will first, not after)?
- How does James describe the attitude in verse 13?
- How about you?

## Cross References

Verses on tomorrow:

Proverbs 27:1 - Do not boast about tomorrow, for you do not know what a day may bring.

Proverbs 3:5-6 - Trust in the Lord with all your heart and lean not on your own understanding; in all your ways submit to him, and he will make your paths straight.

Isaiah 46:9-10 - Remember the former things, those of long ago; I am God, and there is no other; I am God, and there is none like me. I make known the end from the beginning, from ancient times, what is still to come. I say, 'My purpose will stand, and I will do all that I please.

Romans 1:10 - In my prayers at all times; and I pray that now at last by God's will the way may be opened for me to come to you.

## Teaching Points

1. Do not make plans without seeking God's will (13) – The problem is not making a plan. Many verses in the Bible talk about making plans.

Proverbs 16:9 - *In their hearts humans plan their course, but the Lord establishes their steps.*

Creating plans is a way to be organized. Plans can give us a clear goal to work toward. The problem is making plans for ourselves without stopping to consider if those plans match God's plans. The person in James 4:13 is not praying and asking God for direction. He is not saying, "If it is your will, I will go start this business." Instead, he simply makes his plan according to his logic of what he thinks is good for himself. Perhaps later, this person may sprinkle his plan with a prayer and ask for God's blessing.

But making a decision first and then asking God to bless that decision is not the same as sincerely seeking after God's will.

Do you sometimes do the same thing?
Do you sometimes decide first and then ask God to bless it?

We should consider the example of Nehemiah. He heard of the situation back in Jerusalem with the unwalled city in ruins (Nehemiah 1). It was a desperate situation. Instead of immediately rushing to the king with a plan, he prayed and fasted. Only after much prayer, when the opportunity arose (and after another spontaneous prayer), did Nehemiah finally bring a plan to the king (Nehemiah 2).

**Application**: Before making important decisions, stop and pray. In addition, consult other believers who can give godly and unbiased counsel. Do not make any decisions without seeking God; that also means not making any decisions without consulting God's Word.

2. Do not take the future for granted (14) - In the parable of the rich fool, Jesus describes a self-made successful man. He accumulated lots of stuff. He made lots of money. He built lots of storehouses to hold all of his stuff. The man seemed very successful. But he died. And God looked down and said, "Fool." What would he do with all of his stuff? (Luke 12:13-21)

We are not assured another day in this world. We are like a vapor that appears for a moment and then is gone.

**Application**: Because we are not assured of any more time in this world, we should, first of all, be thankful for the time we do have. Secondly, we should use the time that we have wisely (redeem the time by building things for God which will last). Thirdly, we should pray more and trust in the Lord for our future.

3. If it is the Lord's will, we will live and do this or that (15) - We should live every moment depending on God to sustain us and give us success. Never should we take tomorrow for granted. As the saying goes, "Do not count your chickens before they hatch." Making plans without seeking God's will is like this. James calls it "boasting in arrogant schemes." If you are mindful that God is sovereign and on His throne, it will change how you live, face the future, and talk.

Instead of pridefully boasting about your plans, you will humbly trust in God and seek Him each step of the way.

This humble attitude should define all that we do. We should not make promises or guarantees easily since we cannot control the future.

When I tell my friend I will go to his house, I can add "if it is the Lord's will." When you promise to finish a project by a specific date, you can say "if it is the Lord's will."

But much more than the actual words that could become a saying devoid of meaning, we must pay attention to our heart attitude. We should genuinely have this attitude in all that we do. We should be willing to quickly change our life direction if God so wills.

**Point for Discussion:** Share about a time when your plans changed. How did you react? What did you learn?

**Application**: Since time on this earth is short, we should use our time to build God's kingdom. Prayerfully write out a ministry plan detailing some short- and long-term goals of how you will use your spiritual gifts for serving God.

# James 5:1-12

## Outline

I. Rich oppressors will be judged (1-6)
II. Be patient and persevering (7-12)

# I. Rich oppressors will be judged (1-6)

## Discussion Questions

- What is the matter with being rich?
- What position does the Bible teach we should take on money?
- Why would the rich person be subject to miseries?
- Don't rich people normally have fewer miseries than average?
- When will the rich person's riches rot and their clothes become moth-eaten?
- In what way will the rust or decaying of riches be a witness against the rich person?
- How did the rich people in this passage treat their workers?
- What does the Bible say about how rich people, such as employers, should treat those under them?
- Besides mistreating their workers, what other crimes does this group of rich people commit?
- What's the matter with living a luxurious life?
- If you are rich, do you think it is okay to live luxuriously?

## Cross-References

1 Timothy 6:6-10 – But godliness with contentment is great gain. For we brought nothing into the world, and we can take nothing out of it. But if we have food and clothing, we will be content with that. Those who want to get rich fall into temptation

and a trap and into many foolish and harmful desires that plunge people into ruin and destruction. For the love of money is a root of all kinds of evil. Some people, eager for money, have wandered from the faith and pierced themselves with many griefs.

Ephesians 6:9 - Masters, do the same to them, and stop your threatening, knowing that he who is both their Master and yours is in heaven, and that there is no partiality with him.

Matthew 6:19-21 - Do not store up for yourselves treasures on earth, where moths and vermin destroy, and where thieves break in and steal. But store up for yourselves treasures in heaven, where moths and vermin do not destroy, and where thieves do not break in and steal. For where your treasure is, there your heart will be also.

Proverbs 23:4-5 – Do not wear yourself out to get rich; do not trust your own cleverness. Cast but a glance at riches, and they are gone, for they will surely sprout wings and fly off to the sky like an eagle.

Proverbs 28:11 – The rich are wise in their own eyes; one who is poor and discerning sees how deluded they are.

Leviticus 19:13 – Do not defraud or rob your neighbor. Do not hold back the wages of a hired worker overnight.

**Teaching Points**

1. Is being rich sin? - We know from other Scriptures that being rich in itself is not a sin. Sometimes God chooses to bless certain believers with great riches. Abraham, Job, Solomon, and many others were wealthy. Money is neither good nor evil. It is neutral and can be used for good or evil. However, the desire to get rich will ensnare those who have it. Loving money is the root of all kinds of evil (1 Timothy 6:10).

Later in the passage, we will see that desire for more money can lead one to all kinds of sins, including exploiting one's employees and living a life of luxury. James describes the rich as greedy and selfish, loving their money and mistreating others. This is the problem. They were selfish to get more money, and once they had it, they used it for themselves instead of to glorify God, satisfying their own passions (James 4:3).

2. So what is the right view of money? - Firstly, money is not evil, nor is it the key to happiness. It is neutral. There is a right way and a wrong way to get money. There is a right way and a wrong way to use money. Loving money is a sin.

The question is, do you love money? How can you tell if you love money?

Here are a few tests you can use to discern if you love money too much:

- If you find yourself often thinking about money and how to make more money.
- If a major topic of conversation between you and your friends and family is how to make more money or plans on spending money.
- If you often compare how much you make or the number of possessions you have with others, either in pride because you are doing well or envy because you aren't.
- If you are stingy and find it hard to give to God and other people.
- If you love spending money and find a thrill in buying expensive items because you can.
- If at work, you are scheming for ways to get a promotion or always thinking about changing to a better paying job.

The right view is that money is only a tool. It is a tool to provide for ourselves and our families. Nothing more. All that we have is given to us by God. Whatever we have, we should be content with it. It is not sinful to have a plan for the future, either our career or a financial plan or a retirement plan. But as we learned in James 4:13-17 about boasting about tomorrow, it is a sin if God is not in the equation. It is a sin if money itself is our goal. The rich people in verse 1 allowed the love of money to take over their lives and lead them into all kinds of evil.

Because of their lust for money, they were going to face judgment from God in the form of "miseries."

3. Money is temporary (2-3) - It is not lasting. There are no earthly materials or riches that will not fade away eventually.

2 Peter 3:10 - *But the day of the Lord will come like a thief, and then the heavens will pass away with a roar, and the heavenly bodies will be burned up and dissolved, and the earth and the works that are done on it will be exposed.*

Everything you see is temporary. It cannot be taken with you into heaven. If gold and silver can rust and be stolen and fade away, just think of paper money these days. Central governments around the world are printing money and going into record debt. Fiat currency has a one hundred percent fail rate if given a long enough timeline. History tells us that money can lose its value very quickly.

In 1914, about four German Marks equaled one US Dollar. In 1923, 1 trillion Marks equaled one US Dollar. That is not a typo. People had to wheelbarrow around their money to buy bread, and some people even burned it as fuel because it was so worthless.

We've all heard stories of people who lost their fortunes to theft, bad investments, fire, etc. Even if you manage to get through your whole life and hold on to your money, you can't take it with you. What use would US Dollars or British Pounds be in heaven anyway?

James says in verse 3 that "*their corrosion will be evidence against you.*"

Even their rust (decaying, temporary nature) will be a testimony declaring the stupidity of those who place their hope in money. You say, "Yeah, I can't take it to heaven, but I will sure enjoy it on earth!"

But actually, rich people are not really more satisfied or happier than poor people. They always want more, and their riches leads them into many kinds of sins that they wouldn't be exposed to or tempted by if they remained poor.

Proverbs 30:8-9 - *Remove far from me falsehood and lying; give me neither poverty nor riches; feed me with the food that is needful for me, lest I be full and deny you and say, "Who is the Lord?" or lest I be poor and steal and profane the name of my God.*

Riches tend to make people self-reliant and prideful. If God gives them to you, thank Him and then generously use them for His service.

4. The sin of the rich - These people were mistreating their employees. They pushed the workers extremely hard but did not give them a fair salary.

They apparently promised certain wages or bonuses but didn't deliver, unfairly withholding their wages. Making themselves rich on the backs of the overworked, they cared not about the suffering they inflicted on their employees.

This problem exists all over the world. Many bosses care nothing about their employees. They make big promises and don't deliver. Sometimes they refuse to pay what has been fairly earned. The good news is that God knows, and God will judge them for their greed.

**Application:** Christian bosses should take note. You, too, have a master in heaven, and He is watching how you treat your employees. Treat them how you would like to be treated in their position. What is something that Christian employers should do to show kindness to their employees?

5. The sin of luxurious living and wanton pleasure - What is luxurious living? Basically, it is living a lavish lifestyle far greater than what is needed. It is indulging oneself in the lust of the flesh by buying everything possible to satisfy one's wants.

What is the matter with living like this if you have the money?

The problem is that God has given the money to you, and you are a steward of it. Using it like that is a waste.

How can a person excuse using dishes that costs thousands of dollars when there are starving people in the world?

How can a person excuse himself for owning several mansions when there are homeless people in the world?

Sadly, many wolves in sheep's clothes exploit the flock to satisfy their own earthly desires. Some of these have multiple private jets. I have read of one who has a fleet of luxury cars. A lavish lifestyle does not give glory to God. Instead, it is a bad testimony and repels people from the church.

I believe God makes some Christians rich and successful businessmen so that they will generously help support His work. Wealthy Christians should use their riches for God's kingdom and not their own.

Verse 5 says that the day of slaughter is coming. God is going to judge this kind of person, not only the rich person that loves money but anyone who loves money.

**Application:** Spend some time evaluating your lifestyle and your regular giving. Is there anything that needs to be adjusted? Do you need to cut out a luxury so that you can give more?

6. You have condemned and murdered the righteous - James mentions this as the last indictment of those who love money. It is killing the righteous to preserve one's own way of life. Maybe it is a result of overwork or other factors. Certainly, slavery is one example of this happening in history. Many slaves were killed to sustain the lifestyle of their captors.

Solomon's words that "there is nothing new under the sun" are true. History repeats itself again and again. The prosperous either directly or indirectly kill the poor to become richer. Some irresponsible corporations do the same thing today by cutting corners.

DuPont knowingly poisoned thousands of people with Teflon in order to make a profit. Some estimates say that 99.7% of Americans have been poisoned with Teflon. They knew it was harmful and kept doing it because it was highly profitable.

Every rich person who has exploited the poor to enrich themselves will one day face judgment from God.

**Application questions**: If you are rich, what kind of lifestyle should you live and how should use your money? If you are poor, what should your attitude be towards money? How can you guard against materialism? What other Biblical passages talk about money? Why do you think the Bible talks about money so much?

# II. Be patient and persevering (7-12)

### Discussion Questions

- Be patient towards what? Until when?
- What example does James give?
- How can we strengthen our hearts?
- What does it mean that the coming of the Lord is "near"?
- This was written almost two thousand years ago, so how could it have been "near" at that time?
- Does the doctrine of Jesus' second coming and the imminency of his return have any effect on our daily lives?
- Knowing that Jesus is coming back soon, how should we treat others?
- Those who endure what will be blessed?
- What is the other choice besides enduring?
- Why do you think James mentions swearing here?
- What relationship does this have with the prior verses?

### Cross-References

1 Thessalonians 5:14 – And we urge you, brothers and sisters, warn those who are idle and disruptive, encourage the disheartened, help the weak, be patient with everyone.

Romans 8:18 – I consider that our present sufferings are not worth comparing with the glory that will be revealed in us.

2 Timothy 4:6-8 – For I am already being poured out like a drink offering, and the time for my departure is near. I have fought the good fight, I have finished the race, I have kept the faith. Now there is in store for me the crown of righteousness, which the Lord, the righteous Judge, will award to me on that day—and not only to me, but also to all who have longed for his appearing.

Hebrews 10:25 - Not giving up meeting together, as some are in the habit of doing, but encouraging one another—and all the more as you see the Day approaching.

## Teaching Points

1. Be patient - In verse 7, James gives an application to the poor people for the first part of this chapter. They are to be patient.

Maybe we are holding the short side of the stick, meaning we are being mistreated or overworked. What should we do? Go on strike? Demand that justice is done? Complain about our bosses?

We are not to take vengeance ourselves. We are not responsible for their conduct, but we are responsible for our own. We are to be patient with these people and the injustices in the world as we wait for the Lord's return. The illustration of the farmer tells us that this "waiting" period is temporary.

2. Jesus is coming again - At that time, He will judge all those who exploit others, and He will reward all of those who put their trust in Him and respond to these trials in the right way. He says to "strengthen your hearts for the coming of the Lord."

How can we strengthen our hearts? We can turn to His Word. We can be encouraged by the fact that true treasure is stored up in heaven, that true blessing comes from God, that true happiness comes from our relationship with Him, that He loves us, and that He will hold all of these people accountable for their actions.

From God's perspective, Jesus' second coming is near. The word often used in theology is "imminent." That means that it could happen at any time. The coming is inevitable. In comparison with eternity, it is near. The entire church age is the last time period before Jesus' return. It was already near two thousand years ago. And it is certainly nearer today!

3. Do not grumble against one another - All these injustices done to believers by the rich might lead us to complain and grumble. James warns against this by using two-fold logic.

The Judge is standing at the door, meaning He will hold these people accountable for their sins, and He will also judge us if we respond in the wrong way. It should encourage us that the Judge is coming soon, but this is only true if we are doing what is right. Some people think that Jesus' second coming is an irrelevant doctrine, something in the distant future with no relationship to today. To many, eschatology is a controversial topic with no bearing on day-to-day life. But this passage teaches us that that is not true at all. Jesus' second coming motivates us to be patient and respond to trials with trust and perseverance. It has a direct impact on how we live.

Imagine kids are left at home alone, and they know their parents will come through the door at any moment. Will this not affect what they do? Sure, they will want to keep everything straight and tidy and be on their best behavior, knowing that their parents may return at any time. But imagine if they knew their parents wouldn't return for two weeks. Then how would they act? The first thirteen days may look very different from the last. It is possible that they would be a lot looser until the last day, knowing that their parents weren't about to return. On the last day, they would get ready for their parents' return.

But we do not know the day or the hour of Jesus' second coming. So, we need to be ready all the time.

4. Because Jesus' coming is near, we should also endure (11) - James says, "we consider those blessed who remained steadfast." The one who endures to the end will be saved (Matthew 24:13). The opposite of enduring is giving up. We already learned about the test

of trials in Chapter 1. The concept here is similar. The good news for us is that no matter what difficulty we are in the middle of, God loves us. He is "compassionate and merciful" and has good plans for us.

5. Do not swear (12) - James was discussing the coming judgment of the Lord and takes the opportunity to mention, again, one of his favorite topics, speech. He reminds his readers that God will judge all of our speech. Therefore, we must be careful not to swear.

James has taught throughout the book that speech is a window to the heart, a test of our true character. As such, we should know that God is always listening and will hold us accountable for every word we speak.

Let your "yes" be "yes" and your "no" be "no."

The Jews had a habit of swearing deceitfully. They literally had an entire system set up where one kind of oath didn't have to be kept, and another did. For example, they might swear by the food on the altar or by the stones of the temple, but these oaths may not be binding. To the uninformed (likely foreigners), they would naturally believe the oath and act accordingly. Later it would be broken to their hurt, and the one who gave it could just say, "It didn't count." This type of oath is similar to the modern habit of crossing your fingers.

Contracts grow ever more complicated. And unfortunately, the unscrupulous use overly long and complicated contracts to trick people and leave loopholes for breaking their word. Always read the contract before signing your name!

Proverbs 15:4 - *He swears to his own hurt and does not change.*

Our "yes" should be "yes," and our "no" should be "no." That means we don't need to have different levels of promises. Anytime we say we will do something, we should do it even if it hurts and no one else forces us to keep it. If you make an agreement but later find out it is unfavorable to you, do it anyway. You gave your word.

That means we need to be careful before we make promises! This applies to even simple areas of life. When negotiating, don't say the highest you will pay is twenty dollars if you plan to pay up to twenty-five dollars. That is lying. Think before you speak, and remember to consider God's will before making a promise. As we learned in James 4:15, "you ought to say, 'If the Lord wills, we will live and do this or that.'"

**Application:** What is one way you can obey what you learned in this passage and apply it to your life this week?

# James 5:13-20

## Outline

I. Responding to situations God's way (13-14)
II. The prayer of the righteous is effective (15-18)
III. Help the one who is straying to turn back (19-20)

## I. Responding to situations God's way (13-14)

### Discussion Questions

- What are some common negative responses to suffering?
- How should a believer respond to suffering according to passage?
- If we are suffering, what should we pray for?
- Will God always take away the trial from us?
- What is the use of praying if God isn't going to take away the trial?
- What does a prayerful attitude show about our heart?
- What does singing praises show about your heart?
- What is the typical response of unbelievers when they are sick?
- Who are they reliant on?
- What are elders?
- What should you do if your church doesn't have any elders?
- What is the purpose of anointing?
- What are some reasons God may choose not to heal someone?

### Cross-References

On suffering:

Philippians 4:6 - Do not be anxious about anything, but in every situation, by prayer and petition, with thanksgiving, present your requests to God.

Psalms 27:13-14 - I remain confident of this: I will see the goodness of the Lord in the land of the living. Wait for the Lord; be strong and take heart and wait for the Lord.

Psalms 55:22 - Cast your cares on the Lord and he will sustain you; he will never let the righteous be shaken.

On singing praises:

Psalms 105:2 - Sing to him, sing praise to him; tell of all his wonderful acts.

Ephesians 5:19 - Speaking to one another with psalms, hymns, and songs from the Spirit. Sing and make music from your heart to the Lord,

Colossians 3:16 - Let the message of Christ dwell among you richly as you teach and admonish one another with all wisdom through psalms, hymns, and songs from the Spirit, singing to God with gratitude in your hearts.

Other cross-references:

Mark 6:13 - They drove out many demons and anointed many sick people with oil and healed them.

Psalms 30:2 - Lord my God, I called to you for help, and you healed me.
Sin leading to death

1 John 5:16 - If you see any brother or sister commit a sin that does not lead to death, you should pray and God will give them life. I refer to those whose sin does not lead to death. There is a sin that leads to death. I am not saying that you should pray about that.

**Teaching Points**

1. Is anyone suffering? – The word for suffering here is a general word referring to emotional or mental suffering or both, but it is not to be confused with the word for sick in verse 14. In the church, there are bound to be people who are suffering. You likely know people who are facing difficult trials and may be facing one yourself. James tells us how we are to react to that suffering.

If we have any affliction or trial, we are to take it to God to receive His comfort, wisdom, and help. In short, pray. This doesn't guarantee that the source of the affliction will go away, just as Paul's thorn in the flesh did not go away. So, do not let it weaken your faith if you pray for a difficulty to go away and it doesn't.

God doesn't promise to take all afflictions away from us, but He does promise to give us His joy and peace (John 15:11). He also promises to cause all things to work for good to those who love Him (Romans 8:28). Turning to God in prayer shows that we are reliant upon Him. Through prayer, we can align our actions to His will and our attitudes to His desires. Sometimes when the going gets tough, we may give up, complain, or even doubt God. But all of these are sinful, fleshly responses. God is the ultimate comforter and knows exactly what we are going through. We should turn to Him during difficult times. Nothing in the world (chocolate, entertainment, psychologists, or friends) can fully comfort you.

2. Sing praises to God - How about if everything is going smoothly and we are doing well? James says that when you are cheerful, you should sing praises to God. Singing is a way we can respond to God's goodness by proclaiming our thankfulness for His abundant blessings. It shows that we recognize that God is the source of the good things that happen in our lives. Every good thing is from above.

If we are not relying on God, we may forget God during difficult times, thinking that we can "go it alone." We may become prideful, giving credit to ourselves for our good fortune. We may become boastful. All of these are sinful, fleshly responses. In good times or in bad, we need to turn to God and show our reliance upon Him.

3. Interpretative challenge – Starting in verse 14, this is a difficult passage to understand fully. We will take it piece by piece.

**The Problem** - The Greek word for "sick" in verse 14 is "asthenia." This basically means "to be weak," which could refer to spiritual or physical weakness. But another word for sick is used in verse 15, "kamno." This means something like "fatigue." It might describe a book that has been used so much it is worn out. Sometimes it is used for those who are already dead. So physically, it denotes a very serious illness, one which would indicate that death is imminent. This is the problem, extreme sickness.

Furthermore, it is assumed in the passage that the person in question is a believer. This is indicated because James is writing to believers, because the person is under the authority of the elders in the church, because the person is showing reliance on God (verse 13), and because the person would want their sins forgiven (verse 15). This fact makes it very clear that this passage is not some form of the gift of healing where a person is automatically healed as a sign of God's power. Because if it was referring to the gift of healing, anyone could be healed, including unbelievers.

**The Solution** – The sick believer is to call for the elders. This is another indication that his illness is quite severe. Probably he is not very mobile. Elders are overseers in the church. Their responsibility is to shepherd the flock. Qualifications for elders are listed in Titus 1 and 1 Timothy 3. Basically, these are righteous men who live out their faith in God day to day. Because of their upstanding lives, gifts, and role in the local church, they have been recognized as elders.

If a person is critically ill, he should invite the church leaders to come. Note that the sick person takes this initiative. These godly men are then to come and pray over the sick person and anoint him in the name of the Lord.

What is this anointing?

Scripture contains different types of anointing. Often anointing is symbolic as when kings are anointed. Sometimes it was medicinal. Because actual oil doesn't have much effect on many kinds of sicknesses, we can infer that the anointing is symbolic and meant to demonstrate God's healing power and His compassion on the sick. Using real oil would be acceptable to show God's healing power symbolically, but words of comfort and encouragement should also be offered.

It is the elders who pray, and it is their faith that is mentioned as being important. While the sick person has demonstrated a certain amount of faith by calling the elders, not even his prayer is mentioned. It appears that his faith has little to do with the result. So, the sometimes made assertion that "you weren't healed because you didn't have enough faith" doesn't fit with Scripture. If anything, it would be the elders' lacking faith. That is why you need to call for the spiritually mature, not a television healer.

# II. The prayer of the righteous is effective (15-18)

## Discussion Questions

- Does verse 15 guarantee that the sick person will be healed?
- What is a condition?
- Does this mean if you pray for the sick and they aren't healed, it is because you don't have enough faith?
- Why confess our sins to one another?
- Isn't God the one forgives?
- Isn't it enough to confess directly to God?
- Does this passage support the idea of confessing to a priest?
- How do we understand verse 16?
- Do our prayers change things?
- What are some reasons to pray even if God doesn't change His plan based on your prayer?
- What is the danger to our prayer life if we believe our prayers don't actually accomplish anything?
- What does it mean that Elijah had a "nature like ours"?
- What can we learn from the example of Elijah?

- What was Elijah's motivation for this prayer?

## Cross-References

Matthew 17:20-21 - He replied, "Because you have so little faith. Truly I tell you, if you have faith as small as a mustard seed, you can say to this mountain, 'Move from here to there,' and it will move. Nothing will be impossible for you."

Matthew 21:21-22 - Jesus replied, "Truly I tell you, if you have faith and do not doubt, not only can you do what was done to the fig tree, but also you can say to this mountain, 'Go, throw yourself into the sea,' and it will be done. If you believe, you will receive whatever you ask for in prayer."

1 Corinthians 11:30-32 - That is why many among you are weak and sick, and a number of you have fallen asleep. But if we were more discerning with regard to ourselves, we would not come under such judgment. Nevertheless, when we are judged in this way by the Lord, we are being disciplined so that we will not be finally condemned with the world.

1 John 1:7 - But if we walk in the light, as he is in the light, we have fellowship with one another, and the blood of Jesus, his Son, purifies us from all sin.

1 Kings 17:1 - Now Elijah the Tishbite, from Tishbe in Gilead, said to Ahab, "As the Lord, the God of Israel, lives, whom I serve, there will be neither dew nor rain in the next few years except at my word."

## Teaching Points

1. It is the Lord who heals (15) - God's healing power heals the sick and raises him up, not any person's power. The concept of a gift of healing or powerful human healers is nowhere to be found here. God is big and powerful. He still heals people today. He didn't stop doing that at the end of the apostolic age. And God heals sometimes through the prayers of the faithful.

2. If he has committed sins - The phrase "if he has committed sins" is very important and holds the key to the whole passage. First of all, these sins do not primarily refer to sporadic or occasional sins. Rather it references a person who has been persistent and willful in sin. Those are the kinds of sins for which God might discipline by causing the sinner to become sick.

This person's sin will be forgiven, indicating he has confessed and is repentant of his sin. If he wasn't repentant, he wouldn't call the elders since the type of sin in consideration is apparently an open one that the elders would probably know about. One famous scholar who wrote a commentary on the book says it should be translated as, "If he has committed sins, which have given rise to sickness."

In any case, it is apparent based on the context (with sin being mentioned several times) that this sickness is a divine discipline from God for a specific, persistent sin in the believer's life. And when the person in question repents and calls the elders, God will take away the discipline for the sin (sickness) along with the sin itself.

It should be noted that all sickness is not a direct result of sin (as the blind man Jesus healed wasn't in sin).

So. the idea of the passage is this:

A believer has wandered off into sin and remained in sin. This sin has brought about sickness in his life as discipline from God. Once this sickness comes, the believer is to realize it is connected with his sin, repent, and call the elders to help. These elders will come and pray for him. God will forgive the sin, and if it indeed was the cause of the sickness, the sickness will be healed.

3. Confess sins to one another - Verse 16 shows the brotherly love and concern that comes from active Christian fellowship. Confessing your sins to one another is not teaching us we need to have a priest. Only God can forgive sins, and Jesus is the mediator between us and God.

But confessing to one another is a protection as it can offer accountability and enable us to receive help and prayer from other believers. It is also a safeguard to keep us from wandering away from God. We also ask forgiveness from those to whom we have sinned against. The idea is to walk in the light. This safeguard will keep us from reaching the point where God needs to chastise us with His divine discipline.

The verse also teaches us the power of prayer. The prayer of the righteous elder is heard by God, and the sickness is healed. Prayer does matter. God's sovereignty and our prayer are one of the paradoxes of Scripture. God is sovereign and has a perfect plan. Yet He also commands us to pray, and this prayer at least appears to change things. We don't need to solve, and in fact, cannot solve this paradox. We do need to pray righteous prayers out of a righteous lifestyle, full of faith, and believe that God hears and will answer.

**Summing it up –**

1. The person is very ill.
2. The sick person is necessarily a Christian.
3. The sick person is to call for the elders.
4. The elders are recognized leaders of the local congregation who respond to the call.
5. After a time of confession of sin, the elders symbolically anoint the afflicted one.
6. It is the Lord who raises up the afflicted.
7. If the sickness is because of sin, and proper confession is made after the counsel of the elders, in faith we may expect healing. If sin is not the cause, simply pray the desires of your heart, leaving what is best for the individual up to God.
8. The passage does not forbid or preclude the use of doctors or medicine.
9. This passage, under these conditions, is still applicable today.

**Application:** When you are sick, turn to God for help. Evaluate your own life and consider if there is any possibility that the sickness could be due to your own sinful lifestyle. Repent of any known sin and ask believers to support you and pray for you. In turn, you should show compassion for other believers and visit and pray for those who are sick.

4. The example of Elijah – James loves giving examples, and this is an example of a righteous person's prayer and God listening. It is interesting to note that the drought was discipline from God upon a rebellious people. After they repented and turned back to the Lord, this discipline was lifted, and it rained again. Thus, this passage reinforces the conclusion that the sickness was caused by sin and healing was brought about after repentance.

# III. Help the one who is straying to turn back (19-20)

## Discussion Questions

- Who is verse 19 talking about?
- A believer or unbeliever?
- What is our responsibility towards professing believers?
- How can we turn him back?
- Explain the phrase "cover a multitude of sins."

## Cross-References

Matthew 18:15 - "If your brother or sister sins, go and point out their fault, just between the two of you. If they listen to you, you have won them over.

Galatians 6:1 - Brothers and sisters, if someone is caught in a sin, you who live by the Spirit should restore that person gently. But watch yourselves, or you also may be tempted.

## Teaching Points

1. Bringing a sinner back – As believers, we have a responsibility to help our brothers and sisters stay the course. If we see them turning from the truth, we need to share with them from Scripture about what they are doing and encourage them to repent and turn back to the Lord.

Sometimes they might be upset and get angry and offended. We still must do it. Speak the truth in love (Ephesians 4:15). God does not want us to be apathetic to the souls of our brethren!

There are two possible interpretations for these verses. One is that the death is eternal death, "save his **soul** from death." The other is that it is the physical death in mind in the context and that the word for soul can mean something like being, which can also refer to physical death. If physical death was being referred to, it would tell us that God forgives if the person is repentant, even if his sin was severe and prolonged.

If eternal death is what is meant, it would tell us that God will forgive all the sins they have committed if they repent. Since we don't know people's hearts or the state of their salvation, our responsibility is the same regardless.

Either interpretation doesn't affect what we need to do, which is gently but firmly remind the sinning, professing believer to repent and turn back to the Lord.

- Believers are responsible for restoring straying brothers and sisters in the faith. Thus, mature Christian fellowship is a safety net to protect all from falling away from God.
- To continue in unchecked sin can result in death because the believer has disqualified himself from representing God or accomplishing His work.
- Restoration is possible even if the sins are frequent and serious if there is true repentance.

**Application:** When you see a brother or sister in persistent sin, do not turn a blind eye. Pray for wisdom and then approach that person and, through Scripture, let them know their error. If you bring him back, you will save him from death.

**Final Note:** If this study was helpful for you, read more like it on over 30 books of the Bible at studyandobey.com.

Made in the USA
Las Vegas, NV
04 January 2025

15819641R00062